SIMPSON

IMPRINT IN HUMANITIES

The humanities endowment
by Sharon Hanley Simpson and
Barclay Simpson honors
MURIEL CARTER HANLEY
whose intellect and sensitivity
have enriched the many lives
that she has touched.

The publisher and the University of California Press Foundation gratefully acknowledge the generous support of the Simpson Imprint in Humanities.

Coincidences

Coincidences

SYNCHRONICITY, VERISIMILITUDE,
AND STORYTELLING

Michael Jackson

UNIVERSITY OF CALIFORNIA PRESS

University of California Press
Oakland, California

© 2021 by Michael Jackson

Library of Congress Cataloging-in-Publication Data

Names: Jackson, Michael, 1940– author.
Title: Coincidences : synchronicity, verisimilitude, and storytelling /
    Michael Jackson.
Identifiers: LCCN 2020046911 (print) | LCCN 2020046912 (ebook) |
    ISBN 9780520379954 (cloth) | ISBN 9780520379961 (paperback) |
    ISBN 9780520977013 (epub)
Subjects: LCSH: Coincidence.
Classification: LCC BF1175 .J44 2021 (print) | LCC BF1175 (ebook) |
    DDC 133.8—dc23
LC record available at https://lccn.loc.gov/2020046911
LC ebook record available at https://lccn.loc.gov/2020046912

29 28 27 26 25 24 23 22 21
10 9 8 7 6 5 4 3 2 1

The visible is set in the invisible; and in the end what is unseen decides what happens in the seen; the tangible rests precariously upon the untouched and ungrasped. The contrast and the potential maladjustment of the immediate, the conspicuous and focal phase of things, with those indirect and hidden factors which determine the origin and career of what is present, are indestructible features of any and every experience.

—John Dewey, *Experience and Nature*

Contents

Preface

Our lives are, for the most part, made up of unremarkable events. Inevitably, however, the course of every life is punctuated by events that disturb and astonish in equal measure, and when we recount our lives as stories we often single out such events as turning points or moments of truth. This book is about such events. Its particular focus is on coincidences, the "remarkable concurrences of events or circumstances that have no discernible causal connection," and the notions of luck, fate, and providence to which these events give rise. Whether coincidences are construed as fortunate or unfortunate, tragic or transformative, they always evoke wonder and, as the saying goes, "make us think."

As I am writing, my faculty assistant, Andrea Davies, appears in the doorway of my office, and we fall into conversation. At one point, Andrea mentions that she wrote her MFA thesis on James Baldwin's nonfiction and his use of coincidence.[1] When I mention that I happen to be writing a book about coincidence and ask Andrea which of Baldwin's works I might refer to, she suggests I read the opening lines of *Notes of a Native Son*.

> On the 29th of July, in 1943, my father died. On the same day, a few hours later, his last child was born. Over a month before this, while all our energies were concentrated in waiting for these events, there had been, in Detroit,

one of the bloodiest race riots of the century. A few hours after my father's funeral, while he lay in state in the undertaker's chapel, a race riot broke out in Harlem. In the morning of the 3rd of August, we drove my father to the graveyard through a wilderness of smashed plate glass.

As we drove him to the graveyard, the spoils of injustice, anarchy, discontent, and hatred were all around us. It seemed to me that God himself had devised, to mark my father's end, the most sustained and brutally dissonant of codas. And it seemed to me, too, that the violence which rose all about us as my father left the world had been devised as a corrective for the pride of his eldest son.[2]

This coincidence of a personal tragedy and a social calamity prompted Baldwin, "the eldest son," to ponder the connection between his father's generation and his own as well as the connection between the race riots in America and the biblical apocalypse.

Coincidences typically occasion quite different interpretations, and my ethnographic research in Aboriginal Australia and West Africa has taught me that while Western intellectuals tend to refer coincidences to that landscape of shadow that has been termed, directly or indirectly, "the unconscious," preliterate peoples tend to invoke unknown forces like witchcraft and sorcery, lying at the periphery of their social fields. As Michel Foucault observes, the unthought may be construed as deep within "like a shrivelled-up nature or a stratified history" or as something exterior to us, in the penumbra as it were, an "Other that is not only a brother but a twin, born, not of man, nor in man, but beside him and at the same time, in an identical newness, in an unavoidable duality."[3] Although Foucault draws a distinction between the unconscious and the unknown, the former being "an abysmal region in man's nature" and the latter "an obscure space" inhabited by unknown others, he refuses to accord greater weight to either perspective. It could be argued, however, that the dominant episteme since the late nineteenth century has centered on the intrapsychic, not the intersubjective. For Sigmund Freud, as for Claude Lévi-Strauss, delving into the depths of the unconscious mind was the royal road to understanding human thought and action, while Carl Jung interpreted synchronicity as the irruption of archetypal figures and mythological motifs into our conscious life.[4] Although these thinkers evince an intellectual habit that Henri Ellenberger characterizes as "unmasking,"[5] it is practically impossible to sustain any hard and fast distinction between a mode of thought that focuses on the unconscious mind and a mode of thought that focuses on the dilemmas and difficulties of social relations. As Baldwin's compelling account of the coincidence of his father's death and the 1943 Detroit race riots indicates, theological, sociological, and psychological interpretations may all be inspired by the same event. Aboriginal people speak of the Dreaming as an ancestral yet timeless field of being that is occasionally and partially glimpsed by the living in their dreams. For many African people, the mysteries of the invisible can be penetrated by diviners gifted with second sight or assisted by spirit allies. In religions throughout the world, the invisible is a numinous realm to which one rarely gains direct access, though it can be reached by means of prayer, ordeal, and ritual. For scientists, the invisible consists in hidden laws of cause and effect that rational inquiry and sophisticated instruments can bring to light. For many anthropologists, the field of intersubjective life is the subject of their concern: the social matrices in which we are embedded and the dynamic forces that govern our interactions—love and hate, reciprocity and exchange, attachment and separation, certainty and uncertainty, power and powerlessness, war and peace.

What is common to all these interpretive traditions is the mysterious relationship between the visible and invisible dimensions of human existence, the "landscape of shadow" that lies between the known and the unknown and is at once exterior and interior to us.[6] Whether one approaches the phenomenon of coincidence from an intrapsychic or intersubjective point of view, the same assumption is made—that the "obscure space" between the known and the unknown, or between thought and the unthought, can be illuminated, and that the world without and the world within can thereby be seen as one. Methodologically, one therefore needs a bifocal perspective that, in the words of D. W. Winnicott, does justice to the "intermediate area of *experiencing* to which inner reality and external life both contribute."[7] This dialectical approach is also suggested by Carl Jung's comment that synchronicity involves a "peculiar interdependence of objective events among themselves as well as with subjective (psychic) states of the observer or observers."[8] But Jung's fascination with the collective unconscious leads him to downplay the dynamics of intersubjectivity—the passions that unite and divide us, coming together and moving apart in the course of our journeys through life. Historical and even prehistorical events shape our consciousness, to be sure, but we reshape those events in the multiple ways we respond to them after the fact,[9] and any interpretation of a coincidence is inadequate unless it considers the lived experiences and immediate circumstances of those to whom the coincidence happens.[10] Although I do not uncritically embrace either Jung's metaphysical interpretations of coincidence[11] or the Freudian view that our tendency to see meaning in coincidences is an expression of an infantile fantasy of omnipotence (a defense against our anxiety of not being in control of our world), psychoanalysis remains one of the most compelling approaches to understanding "clusters of unexplained facts,"[12] not by glib reiterations of the view that facts speak for themselves but by acknowledging that our evolutionary, genealogical, historical, mythological, and biographical pasts bequeath to us a constellation of elements that emerge in different permutations and combinations at different moments in life, and that our perception of reality reflects these ever-changing assemblages that are never the same for everyone, or for any one person in any given situation. This is why one cannot entirely explain a person in terms of any one variable, be it class, culture, gender, ethnic or religious affiliation, or even personality. This is also why it is imperative to deploy a double perspective that encompasses both the object of experience and the experiencing subject, allowing that human beings are shaped by external forces and conspire in their own fates, seeing the world through the lens of their own preoccupations and interests and creating gods in their own image. One is led, therefore, to broach the philosophical problem of verisimilitude: of speaking truth-to-life, of questioning every truth claim not in order to finally arrive at *the* truth for once and for all but in order to more deeply appreciate the complexity of what is at play for any person, in any moment of time, or in any one place.

TIME TO TIME

A World in a Grain of Sand

Thirty-seven billion years ago, life originated in the ocean depths. Five hundred and thirty million years ago, primitive amphibians found a niche on dry land. As for our species, it emerged relatively recently and may be doomed to become one of the most ephemeral of the myriad life-forms that have inhabited planet earth. It may also prove to be one of the strangest. What other creature entertains the illusion that it represents the highest point of evolution or is supernaturally privileged? Focuses so steadfastly on itself, its immediate environment, and its own kind that it ignores the improbability of its very existence and its dependency on the life of the entire planet. Although we go about our lives in this purblind and single-minded way, we occasionally experience moments in which the wider world breaks in on our consciousness, filling us with wonder or dread and broaching questions about the relationship between our own lives and life itself, between what has been and what may be, and between the world within our empirical grasp and all that lies beyond it. William Blake called these moments "auguries of innocence," encouraging us

To see a World in a Grain of Sand
And a Heaven in a Wild Flower
Hold Infinity in the palm of your hand
And Eternity in an hour

Blake's mystical appreciation of the connection between the great and the small implied both a theology and a theory of social justice, and this becomes very clear as the poem goes on:

A Robin Red breast in a Cage
Puts all Heaven in a Rage
A Dove house filld with Doves & Pigeons
Shudders Hell thr' all its regions
A dog starvd at his Masters Gate
Predicts the ruin of the State

I recently experienced my own auguries of innocence. They came to me as a series of startling flashbacks—of friends I had lost touch with or who had passed away, landscapes I longed to revisit, and wrongs I wished to set right. Although this electrical storm lasted only a few days, it left me wondering if it was a harbinger of death, my whole life passing before my eyes. Yet it was not my entire life by any stretch of the imagination, and as I reflected on the constellation of events, people, and places that had surfaced so abruptly and arbitrarily from the depths of my unconscious, I realized that the question of how one's singular and immediate existence is embedded in social, historical, and macrocosmic contexts had informed almost everything I had ever written.

One of the people who visited me in my dreams was an old friend and erstwhile colleague, Te Pakaka Tawhai. One summer in the 1970s, Paka invited my wife and me to spend several weeks with his family on New Zealand's East Cape. Most mornings, Paka, his father Jim, and I would drive to a shearing shed in the Waiapu River valley where we would spend the day crutching. On our return from work, we would enjoy hearty meals prepared by Paka's mother Pi and his sisters, and in the evening Paka's brother Joe would entertain us with stories.

Paka was keen to show us some of the great carved houses (whare whakairo) of Ngāti Porou, including Te Auau with its calming pastel ambiance and Uepohatu, built under the aegis of the famed lawyer, parliamentarian, scholar, and leader Sir Āpirana Turupa Ngata. On the same afternoon that we visited Uepohatu we drove to Ngata's home at Waiomatatini, where the great man died in 1950 and was buried next to his first wife Arihia Kane Tamati.

After several days and nights steeped in Joe's mythico-histories and now privileged to be shown around "the bungalow" by Ngata's youngest son Hēnare, who took us into his father's paneled study, adorned with the old man's carvings and with his revised Māori bible still on his desk, I was susceptible to a heightened sense that everything around me was charged with significance.

Sitting on the veranda in the late afternoon sun, momentarily alone, I suddenly became aware of the wind rising. Only seconds before, the landscape had been utterly still, but now I was feeling the wind on my face and hearing it ransack the saber-like leaves of the cabbage trees that dotted the plain between the bungalow and the river. At that moment, I experienced the wind not as the wind but as *te hau*, a word that refers to the wind and the human breath as well as the presence of a person of rank and the vital essence of a person, place, or object. I felt I was in the presence of the man whose beloved home Paka had brought us to.

I did not mention this experience to anyone, my wife included, but there were things Paka told me that deepened my sensitivity to the mysteries of Waiomatatini. For several years after Ngata's parents' marriage, they were childless. Following a consultation with a renowned tohunga, Hakopa (of the Te Taperenui a Whatonga School of Learning), the couple was assigned rituals to assist conception. Hakopa also told them that they would have two sons, but when the first was born he would die. "Hakopa knew that by calling on the deities of the ancient world at a time when the beneficiaries of his services had turned to Christianity, his own life was forfeit as utu to give effect to his karakia."[1] The prophecy came true. Not only was an old life taken so that a new life might be given, but the event also signaled that the old order (Te Ao Mārama) was being eclipsed by the new in the same way that daybreak spells the end of the night. Something equally remarkable attended Ngata's death, which coincided, Paka told me, with the clocks stopping in Uepohatu Hall. I did not doubt that this occurred, though it was possible, I later thought, that in the confusion of that time someone forgot to wind the clocks.

Often, it is not an event itself that matters but how we respond to it. Why should we think that the ending of an individual's lifetime entails the ending of time itself, or that the birth of an exceptional individual portends the renaissance of his people?

Having now experienced the deaths of my wife Pauline in 1983 and of Te Pakaka in 1988, not to mention the loss of other close friends, I know that grief can be so devastating that one's own life *does* temporarily come to an end, and it takes time to realize that life itself can and will go on. Something similar happens at a birth. The experience is so intensely intimate that the world around pales into insignificance, and time hangs fire. But then one is struck by the fact that no one appears to have noticed that a miracle has occurred, and one looks for an analogue of one's emotional state in the wider world. If a clock has stopped or appears to have stopped, this means that the world itself has participated in one's joy or sorrow. Objective form is given to one's subjective experience, lending it the wider significance its emotional intensity seems to demand. More importantly perhaps, this search for outward signs that register one's inchoate feelings is the way those feelings become thinkable, manageable, narratable, and shareable.

Our minds are so continually casting about for objective means of giving form to subjective experience that we often overlook the arbitrariness of the words or things we seize on in achieving this goal. As an ethnographer who has lived for long periods of time in remote West African villages, I have had many occasions to remark on the alacrity with which my subconscious would take up local beliefs in bringing a semblance of order to my troubled mind. The question, however, is not whether the beliefs and objects we take up are intrinsically true or false but how they enable us to cope with the exigencies of our situations. This perspective resonates with Susan Lipselter's study of the fantastic and apocalyptic stories people recount about alien visitations and abductions, often in connection with military testing areas. The rage for order that sees coincidences at every turn will readily interpret them as conspiracies and, as with all narratives of minatory power, whether focused on demonic forces, migrants, foreigners, the government, viruses, or UFOs, the recurring leitmotif is an existential crisis of control, comprehension, and certainty.[2] Aristotle used the term *peripeteia* for such confounding experiences in which normal expectations are shattered, our hopes are dashed, and the received wisdom of the tribe proves untenable.[3] Coincidences exemplify these kinds of troubling events and typically lead us to cast about for stories that simultaneously restore our sense of agency and explain the events away.

Usually, these stories are already in circulation, and as Ann Taves observes, we ascribe our inner experiences to preestablished categories such as religion, the unconscious, or the occult, and in so doing confirm them.[4] But our tendency to reify concepts and celebrate stories that prove useful to us, treating them as if they were as real as the experiences they supposedly mirror, does not really confirm their truth, as Agehananda Bharati argues in his work on mysticism. A believer's faith, a mystic's ecstasy, or an atheist's skepticism proves neither the validity nor invalidity of the ontological claims made on the strength of the experiences.[5] Religion is therefore a manner of speaking rather than a sui generis reality. This is why Hent de Vries suggests that we avoid defining religion in terms of "an irreducible realm of being called divine" or as "belief in certain articles of faith, let alone obedience to some ecclesiastical or scriptural authority." Rather, he argues, religion is a semantic strategy for signaling what lies beyond logos ("reason," "word," "rational principle")—things that cannot be directly thought, said, or seen.[6] Mattijs van de Port describes this as "the-rest-of-what-is": "the 'surplus' of our reality definitions, the 'beyond' of our horizons of meaning, that which needs to be excluded as 'impossible,' 'unknown,' 'mere fantasy,' or 'absurd' for our worldview to make sense."[7]

Devaka Premawardhana takes this critique of logocentricity even further by showing how it reinforces structures of social inequality in the Western world. "The most sustained meaning of *logos* in Hellenistic thought," he writes, "particularly that of Heraclitus and the Stoics, is that of a 'unity behind plurality,' the universal ordering principle and law that is as applicable to the cosmos as it is to humans." Premawardhana goes on to argue that the "*logos* (especially its associations with purity and textuality) should be balanced by the *loco*, with its accents on hybridity (*mestizaje*) and orality." It is precisely the possibility of the marginal Latino *loco* de-centering the hegemonic Greek *logos* that will keep theology relevant in an age in which, Edward Said writes, "the huge waves of migrants, expatriates, and refugees ... have become the single most important human reality of our time the world over."[8]

Shifting the logocentric focus of religious studies to what I refer to as *penumbral phenomena*[9] demands new sensibilities, new methods, and novel forms of writing that avoid subjecting these phenomena to symbolic deciphering or mystifying interpretations or using them as evidence for outlandish knowledge claims. A first step in accomplishing this shift is to recognize the mutually constituting dynamic of subjective and objective realities,[10] that is to say, their relational character.

Whether we consider our relationship to the world without or the world within, we confront the same existential dilemma of how best to imagine and manage the gap between these apparently antithetical domains. One of humanity's recurring strategies is to anthropomorphize inner and outer spaces, thereby making it possible to act as if the world in its entirety was governed by the same principles of exchange, reciprocity, and responsiveness that govern everyday social life. This is not to endorse Durkheim's thesis that God is a projection of society writ large. Rather, it is to argue that by assuming that the same laws hold true in both the extrahuman and human worlds, we reduce our anxieties over our ability to control and comprehend forces that lie beyond our ken. In imagining that remote times and places—the depths of the sea, lakes or forests, mountain heights, the heavens, or even distant planets—are peopled by wights, spirits, divinities, and other quasi-human life forms, we close the gap between the familiar and the foreign and open up the possibility of relating to all living and nonliving things as if they shared some common properties. Accordingly, the relationships between inner and outer, self and other, microcosm and macrocosm, and the one and the many are all of a piece. I will argue that this perspective helps us understand why we set such store by coincidences, for they appear to connect our immediate lives and all that lies beyond—the collective unconscious, the realm of the Gods, or simply the life of the world at large.

Lost and Found

When I was nine or possibly ten, my parents gave me a cricket bat and ball for my birthday, inadvertently encouraging my fantasy of one day playing for my school. But it was not in my nature to be a team player and, in any event, I had failed to qualify for the second eleven, even as "twelfth man." I was therefore condemned to hone my cricketing skills by bowling into a brick wall or tossing the ball into the air and hitting it for an imaginary six in the field near our house. One summer evening, as the light was fading, I hit the ball so soundly that it bounced over the boundary of the field and into some long grass. I thought I would retrieve it easily, but the grass was thicker than I had anticipated, and I began to panic. The bad light and my short-sightedness may have led me to mistake the spot where the ball disappeared, and though I bashed at the grass with my bat and stomped about in the hope that I would feel the ball underfoot, it occurred to me that it might be lost forever. Desisting from further effort, I allowed the falling darkness to claim me. I felt utterly alone and completely powerless. The victim of a cosmic injustice that had robbed me of my most prized possession and exposed the hollowness of my fantasy of hitting the winning run for my school team and winning the Ferguson Cup. At that lucid and desolate moment, and without any forethought, I began to pray. I was not religious, though my mother sent me to Sunday School as a concession to her staunchly Methodist parents. One might say, therefore, that the idea of God, like the ideas of gravity, causality, addition, division, and subtraction, had all been seeded in my mind and could, potentially, be accessed and put to use in dealing with any situation in which I found myself.

Though I had never asked God for anything, I now implored Him to help me find my cricket ball.

Almost instantly, or so it seemed, I felt it underfoot. At first, I thought it was a stone. But as I freed it from the entangling grass and passed my grateful hand over its glossy leather surface, I knew that my prayer had been answered.

How was I to account for this coincidence? Had I found God? Had I been favored by a spiritual "gift" or visionary "showing," such as Christian mystics describe?[1]

When I got home and told my parents about the miracle that had occurred, they said they were glad I'd found my ball. When I insisted that God had found it for me, my mother said, "Yes, dear," as if approving my sincerity without confirming my belief.

For several weeks I attended church with my grandparents, though I hesitated to share with them my reason for doing so. Unfortunately, the hymns we sang, the sermons I sat through, and the bible I dutifully read felt quite unrelated to that luminous moment in the dusk when God came to my rescue. Perhaps because I wasn't a team player, or because I was simply too young to understand the arcane texts on which my grandparents set such store, I gave up going to church, and even the memory of that miracle faded, just as the daylight had faded in that unmown field. I had got lucky. That was all.

But was that all?

Why should this event come back to me after being forgotten for so long, like a message in a bottle that crosses seven dark oceans before making landfall? And was this my first inkling of the question that would come to preoccupy me—the question of life unfiltered by logos, and of the sudden irruption of the eternal into the everyday. The question of whether life is a series of accidental and coincidental events or governed by processes that escape the clutches of the conscious mind. Perhaps the question is not one of belief or suspending disbelief but of living with the indeterminate relationship between what we can and cannot know.[2]

In *Memories, Dreams, Reflections,* Carl Jung insists that the only events in his life worth recounting are those in which these mysterious and underlying processes revealed themselves, and he draws an analogy with a plant and its root system that penetrates the ultimate ground of being.

When I decided to re-read Jung's memoir, I could not find it on my bookshelves. Had I lent it to someone, given it away, or lost it during one of my many moves? I was suddenly back in that field looking for my cricket ball. Was it really lost, or had some demiurge conspired to keep it from me?

That these thoughts even crossed my mind bothered me. It was one thing to ponder the philosophical problem of deciding between contingency and design and quite another matter to find oneself entertaining conspiracy theories!

I finally borrowed a library copy of Jung's memoir and located the passage I wanted to re-read.

After discussing what he calls the "natural mind," which possesses an archaic and instinctive gift of seeing beyond the ordinary appearances of people or events, Jung relates an incident that happened many years ago at the wedding of a friend of his wife's. The bride and her family were strangers to Jung, and during the wedding reception he was seated across the table from a middle-aged man who had been introduced to him as a barrister. In the course of an animated conversation about criminal psychology, Jung endeavored to drive home a point he was trying to make by inventing a story. As he recounted this improvised biography, he noticed that the barrister's expression had changed, and that an awkward silence had fallen over the others at the table. Abashed, Jung quickly brought his story to an end and was relieved when dessert was served and he could excuse himself from the table. Minutes after repairing to the hotel lounge to smoke his pipe, he was joined by one of the guests from his table who lost no time in reproaching Jung for his "frightful indiscretion."

"Indiscretion?" Jung asked.

"Why yes, that story you told."

"But I made it all up!"

To Jung's dismay, he had told the barrister's life story "in all its details," though later he was unable to recall anything of what he had said.[3]

How, Jung asks, can one know things one cannot possibly know, at least by ordinary means? And how can one be so profoundly convinced that a story or an idea is one's own when one is sometimes functioning like a ventriloquist's doll, mouthing words that some mysterious other is putting into one's head.[4]

Jung's story strains credulity and raises the question of whether we sometimes trick ourselves into thinking that a coincidence reveals an unconscious compulsion, a supernatural meaning, or a hidden hand operating behind the facade of our conscious life. In short, we tend to select from a constellation of elements those items that confirm our beliefs or support our prejudices.[5] To what extent, then, is coincidence an expression of the kind of wishful thinking that psychologists call "confirmation bias"?

A single detail in Jung's invented story would have been enough to persuade the wedding guests that the stranger at their table was a threat or, for that matter, to convince Jung that he possessed paranormal powers. No sooner have we been captivated by a coincidence than we become alert to others, often considering ourselves prescient when a subsequent event appears to confirm a suspicion or fulfill a prediction. Indeed, having embarked on writing this book I began to see coincidences everywhere. A plane crashes in Ethiopia, killing all 157 people on board. Antonis Mavropoulos, who missed the flight by two minutes thanks to an airline official he had earlier blamed for not ensuring that he got to his departure gate in time, comments that this man "saved my life." But while friends tell him to thank God or his lucky stars, as if he was not meant to die at this time or in this way, Antonis prefers to explain his good fortune otherwise. "I had friends who were travelling and were lost. Everyone at the conference [in Nairobi to where he and his colleagues were flying] is devastated. It's a very sad moment for all of us. It can happen to anyone. It was randomness."[6]

Somewhat the same bemused attitude to fortuity characterizes the story Peter Ustinov tells about the year he won an Oscar for Best Supporting Actor (as Bartiatus in *Spartacus*).[7] Later criticized for not looking surprised when he was called to the podium to receive his award, Ustinov would comment that "though not a believer in the Zodiac and numer-ology...it's been a factor throughout my life that six has been my lucky number. I can't tell you why." He goes on to explain that as the Cadillac in which he and his lawyer were approaching the Santa Monica Civic Auditorium where the 1960 Academy Awards Ceremony was to take place, he noticed a large illuminated sign announcing the Thirty-Third Annual Oscar Awards. Coincidentally, the limo driver had just mentioned that it was his thirty-third birthday. "This is too much of a coincidence," Ustinov told his lawyer. "I've a strange feeling I've got a chance." His lawyer advised him not to get his hopes up; he would only be disappointed if he didn't win, but he does win, and he is not surprised.

Peter Ustinov was a renowned raconteur. Whether one won or lost in the game of life, the experience made a good story. "Everything is copy," as Nora Ephron's mother liked to tell her.[8] For Ephron as for Ustinov, a coincidence was a gift—the gift of a good story. But for Jung, a coincidence is a moment when life discloses its dark secrets, an occasion for serious reflection. In these very different responses to everyday coincidences one discerns the difference between two attitudes toward life, the first informed by a spirit of taking things as they come and enjoying them "for what they are worth," the second characterized by a desire to see beyond the surface of things and explain life, whether in the name of religion or science. Are these alternatives mutually incompatible, or do they both have a role to play in our lives? After all, as George Devereux observes, both Arthur Eddington and James Jeans "concluded from the study of electrons that God exists." However, as Bertrand Russell pointed out, one of these eminent scientists was led to this conclusion by "the 'finding' that atoms *do not* obey the laws of mathematics," whereas the other drew the same inference from "the 'finding' that they *do* obey the laws of mathematics."[9]

Synchronicity and Suffering

When I ask myself why people should assign deep significance to a coincidence rather than brush it aside as inconsequential, I am struck by the degree to which suffering and anxiety increase not only our awareness of patterns but also our compulsion to find them.[1] In a recent report in *Science*, two psychologists at the University of Texas at Austin describe six experiments they conducted in order to test the hypothesis that lack of control increases a person's "illusory pattern perception"—which they defined as "the identification of a coherent and meaningful interrelationship among a set of random or unrelated stimuli." They found that participants who lacked control were more likely to perceive a variety of illusory patterns, including hearing voices in the wind, discerning coherent images in chaotic or scrambled lines, perceiving conspiracies, imagining illusory correlations in stock market information, and developing superstitions.[2]

Speaking of how lives do not end but assume alternate forms, Jung suggests that coincidences often reveal moments in our prehistories, psychic echoes as it were of previous incarnations. "What I found," he writes, "were 'coincidences' which were connected so meaningfully that their 'chance' concurrence would represent a degree of improbability that would have to be expressed by an astronomical figure."[3]

Among the many examples, Jung adduces, is one from Wilhelm von Scholz concerning a young mother who took a photograph of her small son in the Black Forest on the eve of World War I.[4] After leaving the film in Strasbourg to be processed, the woman was distracted by the political turmoil engulfing Europe and was unable to retrieve the film. Two years later, in Frankfurt, she purchased another roll of film, intending to take photographs of her infant daughter. When the film was processed it was found to have been double exposed. To her astonishment the ghostly image beneath the image of her daughter was of her son. For some reason, the film she had deposited in Strasbourg had not been developed but left in its canister and gone back into circulation. For von Scholz, the story confirmed the "mutual attraction of related objects" or an "elective affinity" that unites things or people that belong to each other but have been accidentally separated, like the two halves of Aristophanes's sorb apples.[5]

If there are not only two sides to every story, but two sides to every human being, it is reasonable to ask why von Scholz shows so little interest in the woman who took a photograph of her son on the outbreak of war and two years later recovered the photograph with the ghostly figure of her son underlying the picture of her daughter. This graphic image of one sibling displacing another is compelling enough. But is it not also notable, given the traumatic events that overwhelmed this young mother, that she should crave evidence of continuity in the midst of chaos and find it in this double-exposed photograph? That a coincidence should involve not simply the concurrence of two events, separated in time and space, but also an intersubjective union of two separate lives is not without significance, as the following story, related by my Polish friend Wojcieck Dabrowski, also suggests.

The Dabrowskis had lived in Warsaw for ten generations, and their apartment had been in the family for almost one hundred years. Wojcieck, his father, and grandfather were all born in the same bed, in the same bedroom.

The family's next-door neighbor was a Mr. Zajac—Mr. Hare.

Mr. Hare received a lot of anonymous telephone calls. The phone would ring, Mr. Hare would pick up, and the caller would ask, "Is that Mr. Hare?"

"Yes," Mr. Hare would say, "Hare speaking."

"Pif! Paf!" the caller would exclaim, mimicking a shotgun going off. Then he would hang up.

This went on for several years.

In September 1939, Warsaw was besieged by German panzers and infantry. The city was bombed day and night. Heaps of rubble in the streets, paving stones torn up, gutted streetcars, the stench of burning asphalt and the dead. As fire and panic swept the city, Mr. Hare carried homemade petrol bombs to soldiers engaged in rearguard actions.

For as long as the battle lasted, Warsaw Radio repeatedly broadcast a Chopin polonaise. When the music stopped, the fighting ended. SS units entered the city, arresting and shooting teachers, aristocrats, Jews, clergymen, doctors...

Mr. Hare was taken prisoner only to escape a few days later and make his way to England, where he joined the Resistance. Of his circle of friends, he alone survived the war.

In 1945, he returned to Warsaw. Incredibly, his apartment building was still standing, though for miles around there was nothing but rubble and ruins.

Mr. Hare climbed the stairs to his apartment. The windows were gaping holes. Splinters of glass and chunks of plaster littered the floors.

Over the next few days, Mr. Hare scavenged for food, kitchenware, sticks of furniture. When he discovered that the telephone wires were still intact, he had the phone reconnected.

A week passed, and the telephone rang. Mr. Hare picked up the receiver.

"Is that Mr. Hare?"

"Speaking."

"Pif! Paf!"

Mr. Hare could not believe that this bagatelle, this puerile pun, had somehow survived the years of death and destruction. He implored the caller not to hang up. Mr. Hare was choking with the effort to establish contact. He begged the ghostly caller to reveal his identity, his name, to continue the conversation. But the phone went dead, and the caller never called again.

The Other Portion

It is all too easy to forget that the stories we tell about our lives are seldom entirely true. They are heavily edited versions of what really happened. Accounts of how things should have worked out but didn't. Like dreams that sift through and rearrange the debris of our days in order to offer us the possibility of a new tomorrow, stories sustain the illusion that our lives are within our grasp or, if they are not, then they are in the hands of someone or something that will take care of us. The logic of stories conforms to the logic of logicians only in the sense that everything adduced must add up. But stories rarely reflect our need for incontrovertible knowledge; they answer our existential need to live at peace with ourselves, which is why order must overcome chaos, wrongs must be righted, losses made good, love requited, closure achieved, even though such resolutions are make believe. Even when stories rely on coincidences that are more imagined than real, these coincidences console us that we are not creatures of happenchance and that the pivotal events in our lives were bound to happen and meant to be.

At the same time, it is important to recognize that contingency, unpredictability, and mystery can liberate us from our thralldom to order, exciting us with the possibility that life is a wild ride through a world where anything can happen and in which nothing can be known for certain.[1]

Paul Auster recounts several coincidence stories in *The Red Notebook*, and it was perhaps his fascination with "true stories that sounded like fiction," stories that "defied our expectations about the world, anecdotes that revealed the mysterious and unknown forces at work in our lives[2]," that led Auster to accept an invitation by the hosts of National Public Radio's *All Things Considered* to solicit life stories that could be broadcast on the *National Story Project*. The response was overwhelming. Auster received more than four thousand submissions, and in 2001 he published a selection in *True Tales from American Life*.

The first story in this book had been submitted by a woman adopted from an orphanage at the age of eight months. In her late twenties, she searched for and found her birth mother, now living in Des Moines, Iowa. Her mother helped her track down her birth father in San Diego where, coincidentally, she had been living for the past five years. Indeed, it turned out that she and her father worked in adjoining buildings and often ate lunch in the same restaurant. She later described him as "a bit of a gadabout," though he had been living with his last girlfriend for fifteen years.

"Five years ago," the woman wrote, "my birth mother was dying of cancer in Iowa. Simultaneously, I received a call from my father's paramour that he had died of heart complications. I called my biological mother in the hospital in Iowa and told her of his death. She died that night. I received word that both of their funerals were held on the following Saturday at exactly the same hour—his at 11 a.m. in California and hers at 1 p.m. in Iowa."[3]

I read this story from *True Tales* in a Copenhagen bookshop, but because I could not afford to buy the book, I returned to the bookshop every other day over the next two weeks to continue reading. True though these stories were—in the sense that they set down exactly what an individual remembered about a crucial episode in his or her life—it was clear that what made an event both memorable and narratable was the extent to which it transfigured and redeemed the arbitrariness of existence. For Virginia Woolf, these are "moments of being" when one "sees through the surface to the depths."[4] What moved me about the woman's story of her two birth parents passing away at the same moment, as if their bond had somehow survived their separation and been reconfirmed in the hour of their death, was not the light it cast on the inner workings of *the* world but the poignant insight it gave into *her* world, as if her biological parents dying at the same time answered a yearning in her to be restored to her biological family, her original self. In fact, I would discover that many coincidence stories (including Jung's story of the wedding reception and von Scholz's story of the double-exposed photograph), while ostensibly focused on a remarkable conjunction of *events* in space or time, were allegories of human separation and loss. Oblique or metaphorical commentaries on the hope of repairing shattered lives, the possibility of achieving a transcendent sense of belonging, or bringing together people who had become estranged. It was these dramas of human bonding that imparted to stories of synchronicity their spiritual significance.

So affected was I by the stories I was reading in *True Tales*, and other stories they brought to mind, that I shared my feelings in emails to friends, and that Christmas made a gift of the book to my daughter's partner, thinking it was exactly the sort of book he would like.

The day after Christmas a package arrived by special delivery from Amazon.co.uk, addressed to me. Inside was a copy of *True Tales from American Life*. I inspected the invoice for clues about the identity of the sender. It had been ordered on December 14, and the invoice read "This delivery represents part of your gift. The other portion is being sent separately."

Who could have sent this gift, and what was "the other portion"?

I had told my wife how impressed and moved I had been by Paul Auster's book, so I assumed she must have ordered it for me. The pupils in my son's class at school sent one another small, anonymous gifts at Christmas. Perhaps she was my "Secret Santa."

"No," my wife said, as mystified as I was, "it wasn't me."

I looked forward to finding out, sooner or later, who my "Secret Santa" was and thanking her or him not only for the book but also for the gift of this story that would not be out of place among Paul Auster's *True Tales*. I also wanted to tell my anonymous benefactor that on the same day the book was sent to me, the German writer W. G. "Max" Sebald died in a car crash in East Anglia. Max Sebald would, I think, have appreciated Paul Auster's collection, if only for its lack of literary pretension. For so deeply did Sebald dislike our habit of transforming tragic events into literature that he dedicated his life to creating a form of writing that did justice to the evanescent nature of human existence. If he was reluctant to call his books "novels," it was ironically because he abhorred the "grinding noises" of the genre, with its implausible coincidences, unbelievable resolutions, and superimposed meanings—the very contrivances and artifices without which, it seems, we cannot live.

Correspondences

For two nights, the Night Watch on the battlements of Elsinor has been disturbed by the appearance of a ghostly figure that resembles the late king. On the third night, one of the guards asks Prince Hamlet's friend Horatio to come to the guard platform and see the apparition for himself. Since Horatio is a well-educated man (he studied with Hamlet at the University of Wittenberg), perhaps he can explain the "portentous figure." At midnight, Bernardo relieves Francisco, and shortly after Horatio joins the watch. He is already of the opinion that the ghost is illusory, but on seeing it he is immediately "harrowed by fear and wonder" and now thinks "it bodes some strange eruption to our state." Horatio's intuitions reflect the Elizabethan worldview that cosmic anarchy and corruption in the body politic are closely connected, and his thoughts go back to what he has read of Rome at the time of the assassination of Julius Caesar.

> A little ere the mightiest Julius fell,
> The graves stood tenantless and the sheeted dead
> Did squeak and gibber in the Roman streets
> As stars with trains of fire and dews of blood,
> Disasters in the sun, and the moist star
> Upon whose influence Neptune's empire stands

Was sick almost to doomsday with eclipse.
And even the like precurse of feared events,
As harbingers preceding still the fates
And prologue to the omen coming on,
Have heaven and earth together demonstrated
Unto our climatures and countrymen.

Folklorists have explored the various ways in which untoward cosmic events coincide with aberrations in the social realm. Incestuous unions will be linked to temporal and seasonal chaos ("the time is out of joint") and believed to cause tempests or solar eclipses, according to a logic that equates a wrongful sexual union with an unnatural closeness of sun and moon (often regarded as brother and sister). The same mythological reasoning often connects eclipses with epidemics and cannibalism, which is why disharmony in the heavens is often ritually countered by the discordances of Charivari.[1] In fact, any abrupt change in the cycle of everyday life may precipitate noisy and transgressive behavior, as if a natural connection existed between social life and seasonality, culture and cosmos.

There are echoes of these coincidences between natural and cultural orders in the symbolic connections between our dreams and our everyday lives.

Susan Sontag's 1992 novel, *The Volcano Lover*, is set in late eighteenth-century Naples where Sir William Hamilton is British envoy to the court of the Bourbon monarch Ferdinand IV. Though the novel's focus is the love affair between Emma Hamilton and Admiral Nelson, Sir William's obsessive studies of the volcano that looms over Naples anticipate the violent events that will overtake his private life. In John Banville's review of *The Volcano Lover*, he praises "Sontag's skill and artistic tact" in not laboring "the contrasts between the calmness and frailty of man-made treasures and the unpredictability and chaotic forcefulness of nature, while yet managing to keep this theme firmly in view throughout. In the love that erupts between Emma and Lord Nelson," Sir William "encounters another of those natural phenomena that he can only observe, never experience."[2]

In the same year that Sontag's novel appeared, I met an avatar of Sir William Hamilton in the form of a reclusive New Zealand scientist who, from his teenage years, had been researching the catastrophic eruption of Mount Tarawera in June 1886. Mysterious changes in the water levels of Lake Tarawera and several minor earthquakes preceded the eruption, which cleaved open the earth and covered the land for miles around with millions of tons of volcanic ash, mud, and debris. Ten Māori villages were buried and over 150 people lost their lives.

I met Ron Keam through a mutual friend and became intrigued by his project. At first, Ron was concerned to impress on me the enormity of the Tarawera eruption and the probability that something similar would happen again, only with even more devastating consequences. When I asked him about the phantom war canoe seen on Lake Tarawera by the second-to-last tourist party to visit the famed Pink and White Terraces, Ron said that the sighting was well documented but, as a geophysicist, he did not believe in premonitions. Nevertheless, he had been troubled by his discovery that in the weeks before the cataclysm there had been a mysterious "spate of deaths" that had demoralized the lakeside community of Te Wairoa, soon to be obliterated by the eruption. Even more ominous was the fact that three weeks before the eruption, a high-ranking local chief had insulted one of the "last of the ancient tohungas," a man who had, incidentally, interpreted the spectral war canoe as presaging the destruction of the region.[3] As for the "outrageous affront" the tohunga had suffered, it could only be expiated by death. In cursing the chief who had insulted him, the tohunga declared, "before long something else will happen." The chief, already in poor health, died (of typhoid fever) two weeks before Tarawera destroyed Te Wairoa.[4]

Ron had been fascinated by Tarawera for almost as far back as he could remember. He was an only child and his family often went on excursions to Rotorua where, on one occasion, his father had pushed him into the falling spray of the famed Pohutu geyser. Nor would he ever forget the sulfurous stench in the air and the feeling that the earth was alive beneath his feet, so that "if you trod on one of those little mud volcanoes on the path, the mother of all mud might dump on you in revenge." "My whole obsession, if you want to call it that, is the reliving of that childhood enthrallment, the resolution of childhood puzzles."[5] In the preface to his book, he would write that "from the beginning there was a certain inevitability" about the book being written.[6]

What Ron's childhood puzzles were, beyond an obvious fascination with volcanic and thermal activity, I could only guess. But there were times when Ron seemed to make the Tarawera disaster an allegory of an unhappy childhood. That he spoke of the eruption in explicitly Freudian terms, describing the magma beneath the earth's crust as a seething and repressed force field, made me wonder what lay beneath the surface of his own mild-mannered and rather awkward persona. On more than one occasion he expressed frustration that his research was often interrupted by false trails and unreliable sources. Moreover, he said, "my dreams sometimes get in the way of my work, and there have been times when I have mislaid the negative of a photo or an archival reference only to realize that these items had appeared to me in a dream and did not really exist. Perhaps," he added, "there are some data I so much want to lay my hands on that I dream it, and then lose sight of the difference between what I know and what I am imagining."

Ron planned to write a three-volume work that would revolutionize our understanding not only of the Tarawera eruption but also of the geological vulnerability of the Pacific Rim. I must have made an offhand comment about how deeply invested he was in this project, because a few days later he confided a dream to me in which he was buried alive.

I did not know how to respond to this disclosure, but a few moments later Ron suddenly exclaimed, "I know what that dream's about," and he described his anxiety that after a lifetime's research and writing his magnum opus would not find a publisher, and that his efforts would have been in vain.

In fact, his monumental 200,000-word *Tarawera* was published in 1988 at his own expense, and when asked if anyone would be reading his book three hundred years from now, Ron Keam paused before responding, "Yes. I do believe that."[7]

Certainly, I was incredulous when I discovered that Ron died in the same month (February 2019) that I began writing this book, though I did not know this until after I had retrieved his story from my journal and written this brief reminiscence of my conversations with him thirty years ago.

Ships That Pass in the Night

For three successive summers (2003–2005) my family and I stayed in Zurich where my wife attended seminars at the C. G. Jung Institute as part of her analytical training. Every morning, after she left our apartment for her day's sessions at the institute, I would pack a lunch and take our children down through the beech forest to Küsnacht, where they would buy breakfast croissants and hot chocolate while I ordered an espresso and read the *Herald Tribune*. Our first summer, we spent almost every day at the lakeside, where Joshua and Freya swam and gamboled in the shallows while I read my paper, struggled with the crossword puzzle, or scribbled idle thoughts in my journal.

Every few days, we ventured into the city to buy something to read at the Orell Fuessli Bookshop on Bahnhofstrasse. Joshua and Freya would sit for hours on the couches downstairs, giggling at *Garfield*, while I would sometimes wait for them in a neighboring café, watching the passersby, sipping a citron pressé, or dipping into the novel I had just bought. Toward the end of the afternoon, we would return to Küsnacht by train, trudge up the steep streets of the town into the beech forest, climb the 149 steps that led from the valley to the heights, and walk on through the long grass that fringed the Schubelweiher pond to our apartment. There, the children would write another chapter of their "novels" and illustrate them while I prepared dinner.

Our second Zurich summer was unseasonably cold and wet, and Joshua and Freya were often at a loose ends, unable to summon the effort for a trip into the city and at odds over almost every proposal I made (Freya eager to go down to the lake and feed the ducks, Joshua insisting on a game of football; Joshua desperate to see *Batman: the Movie*, Freya uninterested). One of my last attempts to come up with something that might appeal to them both was a suggestion that we visit the Children's Museum. Though Joshua, in the throes of distancing himself from childish things, understandably rejected the idea, Freya enthusiastically embraced it. The three of us set off for the city anyway, only to fail to find any children's museum on Paradeplatz—the address I had been given by a neighbor. After asking several people for help, I made one last effort to locate the museum, leading my now weary and irritable children down a narrow, cobbled street off Bahnhofstrasse where we came to a building with a blue commemorative plaque on the wall that read *James Joyce Corner*. I was instantly intrigued, but the children were not, and I wound up taking them to *Shrek 2* at the Metropole and afterward to McDonald's. "The day that never was," I wrote selfishly in my journal that evening.

On our third and final visit to Zurich the following summer, I was determined to satisfy my curiosity about Jung's relationship with Joyce and Albert Einstein, who was a professor in Zurich between 1909 and 1910 and again in 1912–1919. Einstein was a frequent dinner guest of Jung's, and it was Einstein "who first started [Jung] off thinking about a possible relativity of time as well as space, and their psychic conditionality."[1]

It was June, already very hot, and Freya was happy to remain in our hotel room watching TV while Josh and I explored the city. To my pleasant surprise, Joshua was fascinated by the history of Zurich, and after taking in the Romanesque Grossmünster cathedral, famous for its associations with the Reformation in German-speaking Switzerland under Huldrych Zwingli (1484–1531), we strolled together along the Limmatquai to Marktgasse as I endeavored to spell out the implications of Zwingli's exhortation that people return to the study of holy writ and the preaching of the gospels and to explain why the reformers stripped the cathedral of everything that gave it a worldly appearance—its pictures, images, sculptures, and musical instruments.

After strolling up one of the narrow streets to our left, we came upon the Cabaret Voltaire at Spiegelgasse 1, where Dadaism was born in February 1916—with its anarchic soirées, its sound and simultaneous poetry, and its transgressive élan. Passing the house of the casuist, poet, and mystic Johann Kaspar Lavater, where Goethe stayed in the 1770s, Joshua and I stopped for a while outside the house in the same street where Lenin lived in exile between 1914 and 1916. I was struck by the coincidences of this period (though could not help but wish Einstein had been in Zurich at exactly the same time as Tristan Tzara, Joyce, Lenin, and Jung), as well as by the incongruities—the Russian exiles toiling side by side with Swiss workers in the local factories (with the exception of Vladimir Ilyich, who was studying in the local library and writing pamphlets against imperialism!), while the Dadaists played their "noise music," donned their bizarre masks, and recited their abstruse poems. This sense of curious juxtapositions was only increased when, the next day, after leaving Josh and Freya to their own devices at the hotel, I made my way downtown to search for the house where James Joyce drafted the early chapters of *Ulysses* in 1916.

It took me some time to locate Seefeldstrasse 54 down an alley off the main street. As I approached the gray stucco, two-storied building, I was no longer conscious of the noise of the trams on Seefeldstrasse or of the ninety years that separated me from the Irish writer's years of exile in Zurich, and I looked up at the windows on the second floor, the window boxes planted with Impatiens, as if Joyce were still in residence. It was close to the middle of the day, the heat was intense, the sunlight blinding. When I saw that the front door was open, presumably so that air could circulate in the stuffy wooden building, I crossed the lane and stepped into the shadows of a narrow hallway, its floor covered with broken linoleum, its lower walls paneled with wood that had been painted cream. Everything about the place was consistent with what I had read of the penury and shabbiness of the Joyce family's life in their damp, two-bedroom flat at this address, and it was easy to understand why Joyce spent long evenings in cafés and restaurants, including the nearby Club des Étrangers on Seefeldstrasse.

After leaving Zurich, I found myself wondering whether these famous exiles, Joyce, Lenin, Jung, and the Dadaists, ever met and, if they had, what they had thought of one another. Apparently, Joyce and Lenin had both been regular customers at the Café Odeon in Spiegelgasse, and on the one recorded occasion that their paths had crossed, the Russian opined that the Irishman was "a great personality." As for Joyce and Jung, they never met face to face until, a decade later when, desperate to find help for his mentally ill daughter Lucia, Joyce briefly entrusted "his 'yung' daughter so 'easily freudened,' to the ministrations of the 'grisly old Sykos.'"[2] But his attitude toward Jung was negative from the start, and he described Jung as "the Swiss Tweeldedum" and Freud as "the Viennese Tweeldedee," amusing themselves "at the expense (in every sense of the word) of ladies and gentlemen who are troubled with bees in their bonnets."[3] As for Jung, he would dismiss *Ulysses* as boring and wonder how anyone could "go through the book from page 1 to page 735 . . . without fatal attacks of drowsiness." After his one meeting with Joyce, in the course of treating Lucia, he concluded that both father and daughter were doomed, "like two people going to the bottom of a river, one falling and the other diving."[4] Joyce's reaction was to ask himself how a person who misconstrued *Ulysses* could possibly understand Lucia, and he rejected Jung's suggestion that Lucia was his *anima inspiratrix*, the implication being that he was exploiting as grist for his literary mill a family tragedy.

One of the lines of research I pursued concerned the month of February 1917, when news of the revolution reached the Russian exiles in Spiegelgasse. What, I wondered, were Jung, Joyce, and the Dadaists doing as Lenin and his comrades packed their bags and tried to figure out how best to return to Russia? That month, Tristan Tzara published one of the first issues of the periodical *Dada*. As for James Joyce, he contracted glaucoma, his *Portrait of an Artist as a Young Man* came out in England, and his first significant patroness, Harriet Shaw Weaver, began her financial support of the penurious writer. Jung was writing *Psychological Types*.

I suppose one could classify all these figures as "introverted thinking" types, but such discursive summarizing obscures the great differences between their various commitments, to revolution, to art, and to understanding. And any attempt to find some "acausal connecting principle" of synchronicity, revealing a pattern beneath the temporal and spatial coincidences that all of us, now and then, are momentarily struck by, seems somehow beside the point when the overwhelming evidence is not only of contingency and disconnectedness, but of the miraculous appearance of something new in every encounter that makes it impossible to precisely predict the future or reduce the present to the past, yet offers us the perennial possibility of redemption.[5]

Chance Meeting

Zurich's Fluntern Cemetery was under snow. Only the main path, leading slightly uphill from the main gate, had been cleared. After examining a notice board that showed the layout of the cemetery and identifying the numbers of some of the more famous graves, I followed a well-trampled path between serried gravestones, amazed to see how many footprints there were, though not a soul was in sight. Joyce's grave was the first I found. His statue was encrusted with snow—the gangly, self-absorbed figure with cigarette and cane almost a caricature of the heroic individual I had conjured when I read his work as a young man. A few feet away I found the snow-obscured, less visited grave of Elias Canetti. Someone had placed a Chinese candle on the grave, protected from the weather by a crimson tube with gold filigree. Judging from the snow around its base, it had been set there before the recent snowstorm. Sweeping the snow from the grave with my gloved hand, I then used my ballpoint pen to dig snow out of the spidery holes in the brass slab, deciphering Canetti's signature. Nearby was a stand of cedars overburdened by snow. I heard the caw of a rook, a snatch of distant voices, and the hum of traffic before the snowbound muffling silence reclaimed the place and I was alone with my thoughts.

In 1968 my first wife and I were living in Wellington, completing our master's degrees before taking up scholarships at Cambridge. Our landlady, Kay Miller, was an eco-activist who had gotten media attention for building a hut on the Porirua rubbish dump from where she supervised a recycling project and campaigned against the pollution and desecration of the environment. Kay would make us salads from edible weeds, to be washed down with her home-brewed dandelion wine, and she would regale us with stories of her student days in London when she had formed a close friendship with Elias Canetti. When Pauline and I left for England, Kay entrusted us with a package that we were to deliver into the hands of her longtime friend in Hampstead. The package contained copies of correspondence between Kay and Canetti, possibly for use in the memoirs Canetti had begun to write. In any event, Kay impressed on us the importance of the documents and the absolute necessity of delivering them to Canetti by hand. In 1968, I had read nothing by Canetti and was unaware that Veza (Venetiana Taubner-Calderon), his wife and literary collaborator, had died in 1963. So when Pauline and I went to the address that Kay Miller had given us and rang the doorbell, we did not know whether the woman who opened the door was a wife, research assistant, housekeeper, confidante, or passing acquaintance. What was made very clear to us, however, was that Canetti was not to be disturbed. She, whoever she was, would ensure that Kay's precious package was safely delivered to him. There seemed no alternative but to give her the package and leave. But our failure to fulfill our promise to Kay weighed on our minds and led me to ask who this man was, sequestered in this grand Victorian house in Thurlow Road, not far from where Freud had lived, a neighborhood where almost every home was associated with "the guttural sorrow of some famous émigré intellectual, or the names of legendary English poets."[1] When Canetti and Veza observed the Battle of Britain from Hampstead Heath, "they probably stood in almost the same spot as D. H. Lawrence and Frieda, who in 1915 had watched a German Zeppelin attacking London."[2]

In *Crowds and Power*, Canetti writes that "it is not always veneration for some famous man" that draws us to cemeteries. "Even where this is the original motive, the visit always turns into something more."[3] This remark proved prescient.

After locating the grave of the man I had narrowly missed meeting over forty years ago, I attempted to write down my thoughts, but the pen with which I had traced the cutout letters of Canetti's name had seized up. Canetti, however, had anticipated my own reflections in a posthumously published collection of autobiographical writings that includes a brief essay on the Hampstead Parish Church cemetery where John Constable is buried. Some of the graves in the churchyard date to the seventeenth century when Hampstead was a minor spa on a hill north of London. Canetti says it was not until late in his life that he "learned what cemeteries are." He speaks of the gravestones, half sunk in the ground or standing askew with their weather-eroded dates and names, as offering themselves to be gazed on, and of the "peaceable feeling that comes on you from this elementary act of looking at the stones. Standing there, mindful of the passage of time that stands between you and your predecessor, is a kind of homage." "You read his name, you perhaps spoke it half-aloud to yourself, you had no reason to bear him any ill-will, and if you didn't feel gratitude to him as such, you did, in a simple, natural way let him participate in the time in which you were contemplating him. It may sound strange, but it helps to explain the warm feeling you had, when you came up to some of these stones, and gazed at them, as if you had known the people."[4] Canetti goes on to say that after his frequent visits to the Church Row cemetery he felt that he had discharged a debt. But he leaves open the question of how one might explain this sense of owing something to the dead, whether it be recognition or care or an acknowledgment of our common mortality.

The dark green cedars were deathly still, and a milky sun showed through laundered layers of cloud as I returned to the main path, reluctant to leave the cemetery, as if an experience I had expected had been denied me, or I was deserting someone who had placed his trust in me.

At that moment, I noticed a young African man standing in front of a large gravestone. He was wearing a knitted skullcap and black woolen overcoat, and I was struck by his stillness and concentration. His only movement was to gently stab his Blackberry with a stylus as if texting or taking notes. As I walked past him, our eyes met, and there was a flicker of mutual recognition. Stealing a glance backward, I tried to decipher the names on the gravestone, intrigued by what connection this visitor had with the four family members buried there. The farther I went toward the main gate, the more my curiosity increased. I could not leave the cemetery without knowing more or coming up with a satisfying fictional answer to the question that now bothered me. I wandered slowly around the perimeter of the cemetery, assuming he would soon end his vigil and I would be free to examine the names on the gravestone. Five minutes later he was still there, a short dark contemplative figure in the snow, as improbable and provocative as an apparition. I could curb my curiosity no longer. Sidling up to him, I asked if he spoke English.

"Yes."

"Do you mind me asking, what is the connection between you and the names on that grave?"

"I am Opus Dei," he said. "We are working for the canonization of Toni Zweifel."

He was a student in Geneva, finishing doctoral studies in biotechnology. He had come to Zurich for an Opus Dei retreat. They were praying for Zweifel's beatification, and praying for peace.

I asked where he was from.

"Côte d'Ivoire," he said.

Only that morning I had read the latest news from Ivory Coast—the growing violence between the followers of the former president, Laurent Gbagbo, and the president-elect, Alassane Ouattara, and the thousands of West African immigrants already fleeing the country, fearful of the threats being made against them.

"What of your family?" I asked. "Are they safe."

"They are safe. I am praying for them. And for my country."

"What is the root of the conflict?" I asked.

"International interference. The colonial powers don't want to give up their interests in Côte d'Ivoire."

We strolled to the tram stop together. He asked where I lived and what I did for a living. I told him I taught anthropology at Harvard Divinity School. I could see he took a dim view of anthropology, but he brightened at the mention of Harvard and asked for my card. When I explained that I did not carry a card, he entered my address into his Blackberry. "God brings people together," he said. "There is always a reason."

He then asked if I was a Catholic.

"No, I adhere to no faith."

I presumed he would board the tram with me, but as it pulled in he extended his hand to say goodbye.

"I hope your prayers are answered," I said.

He looked at me as if an atheist could know nothing of the power of prayer. Then he smiled.

I smiled too, descending the long hill back to Zurich in the tram and writing notes on our brief conversation. I had made a pilgrimage to the graves of two writers, believing nothing much would come of it, only to be surprised by an encounter that lay in wait for me, as it were, only yards away. And where my relationship with Joyce and Canetti had not produced any epiphany, I had witnessed in this other pilgrim's devotion to a Swiss engineer, whose Limmat Foundation supported hundreds of educational and social service initiatives in more than thirty countries on five continents, a connection that was as spiritual as mine was casual. Did I envy this young African his passionate campaign to have Toni Zweifel recognized as a saint or, for that matter, his depth of commitment to Opus Dei, his sense of divine purpose, his cause? There seemed, when I reflected on it, too much contingency in life to allow for this kind of clarity. And this was brought home to me when I returned to my hotel in Hottingenstrasse and discovered, via the internet, that both of Toni Zweifel's parents died within three months of each other in 1985, and that a year later Toni learned that he was suffering from leukemia, for which he underwent chemotherapy. After a temporary return to health, he suffered a first relapse in February 1988 and a second the following November. In June 1989 he was hospitalized for further treatment, but he died that November, age fifty-one.

Coincidence and Theodicy

Thornton Wilder's half-forgotten masterpiece, *The Bridge of San Luis Rey*, begins with a tragedy that seems to defy explanation. A rope bridge gives way as a group of travelers are crossing a deep ravine, and they are thrown to their deaths. A Franciscan priest who witnesses the accident is both stunned and mystified. *The bridge seemed to be among the things that last forever; it was unthinkable that it should break*. How could a benevolent God allow this fate to befall innocent people? There must surely be some reason for their deaths. *Why did this happen to those five?* Wilder's book recounts Brother Juniper's attempts to research the back stories of the victims and arrive at a theologically meaningful explanation of why they should have died at that time, and at that place.

For those who repudiate the idea of divine omniscience and design, it is still not easy to accept that life may be devoid of ultimate meaning, and that accidents happen for no good reason. Though we may receive windfalls without much questioning, ill fortune tends to provoke considerable soul-searching. It seems outrageous, for example, that a young and beautiful woman should die of cancer, or that a brilliant writer, at the height of his powers, should perish in a car crash, while a corrupt tyrant enjoys health and happiness. Surely life is more than a lottery. Surely the good do not deserve to suffer and evil go unpunished. Surely there is some reason why some of us should live in hell, while others inhabit paradise.

For John Dewey, both science and religion ultimately founder on the same problem of understanding why things happen as they do, and how we can make things happen as we wish them to. Early anthropologists like Edward Tylor characterized "primitive" thought and ritual as obsessively concerned with the causes underlying unforeseen or calamitous events. To assign a cause gives one a sense of magical mastery over nature, just as a belief in God as primum mobile may assure us that an omniscient Being will prevent the world from descending into complete chaos. In the nineteenth century, the notion of statistical laws mitigated the fear of pure randomness, not in the sense that chance "could be controlled but in the sense that it could be subjected to calculation."[1] Where people had once been fascinated by coincidence and fate, rational inquiry now focused on the methodical search for statistical correlations. These various strategies for "taming chance" might not forestall misfortune, but at least they helped explain the phenomenon. As Brother Juniper's search for meaning in the aftermath of an inexplicable tragedy reminds us, all human beings find it difficult to accept a world governed by chance in which the forces of nature or the whims of the gods appear indifferent to the social and moral rules that govern human life.

But if meaningful patterns can sometimes be glimpsed in what at first sight are random occurrences, can chance be made to serve rather than confound us?

Consider divination in West Africa, where a jackal's footprints across a sand diagram[2] or a diviner's intuitive placement of pebbles in groups of two or three will be read as signs of imminent good or ill in a client's life. For Kuranko, it is less important to understand the past than anticipate and influence the future. This requires offering sacrifices to ancestors, djinn, and mentors. But only a diviner can tell exactly what sacrifices have to be made, and to whom. Guided by spirit allies or by God, he alone can "see" how a client may avert misfortune or ensure an untroubled future. That external powers and supernatural agencies are invoked does not mean that Kuranko are fatalists, for it is, paradoxically, through acquiescence to the powers-that-be that clients recover their ability to act decisively and with confidence. In other words, randomness is a ritual means for discerning underlying order and acting in accordance with it. Magic entails, therefore, not an abnegation of the will but a means of distancing or disengaging oneself from subjective confusions and anxieties, the better to recover a sense of control over one's life.[3]

For Dewey, we are so continually coming up against the limits of what we can comprehend and control that uncertainty is "a primary datum in any experience," and though "our magical safeguard against the uncertain character of the world is to deny the existence of chance, to mumble universal and necessary law, the ubiquity of cause and effect, the uniformity of nature, universal progress, and the inherent rationality of the universe . . . when all is said and done, the fundamentally hazardous character of the world is not seriously modified, much less eliminated."[4] Even so, surely it is important to recognize the ways that human beings act *as if* they were not at the mercy of chance and circumstance?

In his highly regarded study of witchcraft and oracles among the Azande of the southern Sudan and northeastern Congo, the British anthropologist Edward Evans-Pritchard documented this quest for certainty in a world of chance.

In Zandeland sometimes an old granary collapses. There is nothing remarkable in this. Every Zande knows that termites eat the supports in course of time and that even the hardest woods decay after years of service. Now a granary is the summerhouse of a Zande homestead and people sit beneath it in the heat of the day and chat or play the African hole-game or work at some craft. Consequently, it may happen that there are people sitting beneath the granary when it collapses and they are injured, for it is a heavy structure made of beams and clay and may be stored with eleusine as well. Now why should these particular people have been sitting under this particular granary at the particular moment when it collapsed? That it should collapse is easily intelligible, but why should it have collapsed at the particular moment when these particular people were sitting beneath it? Through years it might have collapsed, so why should it fall just when certain people sought its kindly shelter? We say that the granary collapsed because its supports were eaten away by termites. That is the cause that explains the collapse of the granary. We also say that people were sitting under it at the time because it was in the heat of the day and they thought it would be a comfortable place to talk and work. This is the cause of people being under the granary at the time it collapsed. To our minds the only relationship between these two independently caused facts is their coincidence in time and space. We have no explanation of why the two chains of causation intersected at the certain time and in a certain place, for there is no interdependence between them.[5]

The Zande problem, as Evans-Pritchard presents it, resembles the problem of theodicy that vexed Leibnitz and Brother Juniper. Though Leibniz speaks of *malum* (evil) and the Zande speak of *mangu* (witchcraft), both words suggest that the course of human life is unpredictably interrupted by events that seem inexplicable and unjust, and, moreover, call into question the point of living a blameless social or ethical life if this does is not rewarded by happiness. Must we accept that we live in the best of all possible worlds, and that neither religious faith nor scientific knowledge can offer us certainty and security?

What fascinates me about Zande philosophy is that it does not seek evidence for divine or natural laws but looks for evidence of human malice. That is to say, Zande are less concerned with *what* caused the granary to collapse than with *who* is to blame. The explanation for the coincidence between the moment that certain people were sitting beneath the granary and the moment its supports gave way is witchcraft. "Witchcraft explains the coincidence of these two happenings."[6] It does not eschew empirical observation and reasoning; rather, it ascertains whether termite damage or human malice was the *principal* reason, the *primary* cause, of the granary's collapse. Zande use hunting parlance to make this point. When an animal is brought down in a hunt involving several hunters, the division of the meat will be decided by who threw the spear that inflicted the mortal wound. In the face of catastrophic events, postmortems, legal processes, second-guessing, and divination may all play their part in arriving at a consensus about the relative weight of several factors in causing the event to occur: to decide between the first spear and the second spear.

But what do these questions tell us about the immediate experience of those who lose a loved one in a tragic accident? What is the relationship between explaining an event and surviving it—between verisimilitude as speaking truth to the facts or speaking truth to experience? In addressing this question, it is imperative that we see experience relationally since coincidences, like any other phenomena, are at once *external* events that impress themselves on our consciousness *and* ex post facto constructions that reflect learned predispositions for organizing our perceptions in certain ways. What we call *reality* is always an emergent property of this relationship between perception and conception.

On May 31, 1970, the worst recorded natural disaster in the western hemisphere befell the inhabitants of a remote Peruvian valley in the Andes, and 75,000 people in the Callejón de Huaylas lost their lives.

A graduate student of anthropology who was looking for a site to do fieldwork at this time heard news of the disaster and felt moved to respond. Only months before, she had lost the child she was carrying, and felt "awesomely free... shaken like the glacial valley I had heard about on the radio.... I needed to do something extraordinary to catapult myself out of my personal tragedy. So I went to that Peruvian valley... and spent a year there that forever marked my life."[7]

When I read Barbara Bode's book I was not only struck by the interplay of her own private trauma and the earthquake itself (a friend in Huaraz told her she had suffered an earthquake inside her[8]), but also by the ways in which survivors searched for clues about why this had happened, at that time, in that place, to them. This search for the tragedy's "ultimate cause"[9] involved both subjective and objective conceptions of the truth. At the same time that individuals searched their souls for answers, they shared a common desire to identify objective causes. One woman asked how she came to be out in the open when the earthquake struck, then explained that she was about to take part in a religious procession and her devotion to her ritual obligations had saved her life.[10] Others spoke of auguries of what was about to happen, signs they had misread or ignored. Many explained the tragedy as divine punishment for sins and a reminder of God's power. Others spoke in political terms, arguing that the cataclysm was a "providential mandate" for social reform, or even revolution.[11] And while most people accepted scientific explanations of the region's proneness to earthquakes, many saw the disaster as having been "provoked" by the landing of human beings on the moon and the French testing of atomic bombs in the Pacific—signs of human assaults on the earth's natural order.[12]

Despite the diversity of these conjectures, one common thread can be discerned in all of them: nothing happens by chance. It is as if the idea of chance is almost as unbearable as the loss of life. Which brings me back to Barbara Bode's reflections on her fieldwork in Huaraz and the ways in which life always involves deep connections between external circumstances and personal preoccupations.

"My fieldwork in the Callejón," Bode writes, "was in part an attempt to propel myself worlds away from my personal tragedy, to globalize it by living it through within a much larger context. Earthquake survivors, too, broadened their sights, projected their personal and community tragedy against a world screen."[13]

I hesitate to speak of projection here, for the world impinges on us to the same extent that we respond to it. The relationship is always two way, and the meanings that emerge from these interactions are always indeterminate, which is to say they cannot be reduced either to the experiencing subject or the object that is experienced. Werner Heisenberg called this the uncertainty principle. Yet one of the greatest minds of the twentieth century resisted its implications. In a letter to Niels Bohr, Einstein wrote, "Quantum mechanics is very impressive, but I am convinced that God does not play dice."[14]

Amazing Grace

When I returned to Sierra Leone at the end of the civil war in January 2002, many villagers were struggling not with traumatic memories, nor with questions of reconciliation or revenge, but with finding food, medicines, shelter, and seed rice with which to rebuild their lives. Explaining the causes of the war and understanding rebel atrocities were luxuries the poor could ill afford, and I was moved, as I had been in the past, by the stoicism and silence with which people endured the tragedies that befell them. Indeed, the Object Lesson of initiation, when pain is deliberately inflicted on neophytes, is that one thereby acquires the virtues of fortitude and imperturbability without which the tribulations of life will be insufferable. Pain is an unavoidable fact of life; it can neither be abolished nor explained away. What matters is how one endures it. This implies an ability to not dwell on the past or expect a brighter future, but rather to make the most of what one has in the here and now.

But does accepting one's lot extend to accepting chance, or accepting that one is sometimes powerless to determine one's own fate?

In the course of a long day in one of Freetown's amputee camps, a young Kuranko woman ended her harrowing story by reminding me that there was nothing she could do to redress the damage that had been done to her. When, a few days later, I shared Fina Kamara's comments with my friend Noah Marah, he said, "It's what you might say when someone offends or hurts you, and you are powerless to retaliate. If, for instance, someone takes something from you without justification. Or insults and humiliates you for no good reason. Say a hawk came out of the blue and seized one of your chickens. What can you do? You can't get it back. The hawk has flown away. You have no means of hunting it down or killing it. All you can do is accept and go on with your life. But you don't really forgive, you don't really forget. You simply accept that there's nothing you can do to change what has happened. Look at me. I have no way of taking my revenge on the rebels who took away my livelihood, but at least I can rid myself of them. I can shut them out of my mind. I can expel them from my life."

Noah's words reminded me of a passage in Hannah Arendt's *The Human Condition*.[1] Forgiveness implies neither loving those who hate you, nor absolving them from their crime, nor even understanding them ("they know not what they do"); rather, it is a form of redemption, in which one reclaims *one's own life*, tearing it free from the oppressor's grasp, and releasing oneself from those thoughts of revenge and those memories of one's loss that might otherwise keep one in thrall to one's persecutor forever.

"If I say *i hake a to nye*," Noah continued, "I am freeing myself of the effects of your hatred. I am refusing to hate back. But this doesn't mean that justice will not be done. Most of us here feel that God sees everything, and that God will mete out punishment in His own good time. That's why we say, *Alatala si n'hake bo a ro*, God will take out my anger on him. So I might say, *m'bara n'te to Al'ma*, I have left it up to God. Same as they say in Krio, *I don lef mi yon to God*. I think this is what Fina Kamara meant. She was not saying that she forgives the rebels, but that she is leaving it up to God to see that justice is done. Because how can you ever be reconciled to someone who has killed your father or cut off your hand? Reconciliation, forgiveness, forgetting . . . these are all relative terms. In Sierra Leone right now, we are letting sleeping dogs lie. You understand? We are fed up with the war. Fed up with atrocities. If we talk about the war, it is not because we are plotting revenge or want to prolong the suffering. We simply do not want it to happen again."

Noah's observations brought home to me the difference between what Veena Das calls cosmologies of the powerless and cosmologies of the powerful.

Cosmologies of the powerless hold the capriciousness of god and the sheer contingency of events responsible for the disorder of their lives; this, at the very least, has the potential of freeing those who suffer from having to take personal responsibility for their fate.... But in the cosmologies of the powerful, conversely, there is no place for chaos. For if the contingent and chaotic nature of the world were acknowledged in these, it would have the potential to dismantle the structures of legitimacy through which suffering is imposed on the powerless.[2]

While ordinary Sierra Leoneans resisted the implementation of a Truth and Reconciliation Commission on the grounds that it would open old wounds and cause further suffering, Western authorities, certain in their knowledge of what was necessary to secure justice, imposed their will on the powerless. Justice could not be left to God. The Western powers, that had invoked divine right in their colonization of Africa, now repeated the same performance, abrogating the power of God in the guise of human rights to justify their intervention.

These thoughts were weighing on my mind when, crossing the Aberdeen Bridge one evening with my friend Sewa Koroma, we stopped to look across the tidal flats where women and children were searching for shellfish. Suddenly, several images converged in my consciousness, connecting this present moment with the past.

Several years ago, I had sat on the balcony of the house of two close friends, S. B. Marah and his wife, and looked out over this same scene. "Did I know," Rose asked, "that the real name of the bay wasn't Thompson's but Thousands, because it was from here that the slave ships set sail for the Americas with their human cargos?"

"I didn't know," I said.

"Yes," Rose said. "They used to ship slaves from this inlet."

I remembered the old university building in Cline Town, built from the timbers of captured slave ships, iron ring bolts still embedded in the walls.

"Thousands of them were herded into caves and barracoons," Rose said, "before they were taken out to the ships offshore."

Suddenly, Sewa broke into my reverie, telling me that scores of rebel soldiers were brought to the bridge in January 1999, summarily shot, and their bodies thrown into the bay.

As the bluish twilight settled over the mangroves, the mudflats, and the sinuous channels of water beneath us, I found myself thinking how easily scenes of horror and tranquility succeed each other on the same stage, and I recalled Marlowe's words in *Heart of Darkness*, as he and his companions watched the light fading on the sea-reach of the Thames: "And this also has been one of the dark places of the earth."

The barracoons were slave pens built on the beaches. Coffles or trains of slaves were brought to the coast from up-country, roped together at the neck with leather thongs. All were forced to carry headloads of ivory or food. All bore welts and scars from lashes and chains. The sick and exhausted were shot.

On the coast, men, women, and children were stripped, and further selections were made by the slave master and his "surgeon" to ensure that sick individuals would not contaminate the healthy on the voyage out. Two days before shipment, the heads of the slaves were shaved. Sometimes they were branded on the arm with the initials of the merchant to whom they now "belonged."

In Sierra Leone, the slave ships anchored offshore and the slaves were brought out to them in longboats. Two hundred and fifty people would be "tight-packed" on three tiers or shelves in a hold with a six-foot ceiling. No individual had a space of more than six feet by sixteen inches in which to move. It was impossible to sit upright, and people were handcuffed and leg-ironed in pairs, "the right hand and foot of one to the left of the other, but across," so that no one could move without disturbing the person to whom he or she was shackled. Sometimes it was worse. Up to 750 men might be "stowed in each other's laps" in a three-foot space between decks, "without an inch to move right or left," and, in a partition of the bulkhead measuring sixteen by eighteen feet, 250 women, some pregnant, would be confined.

In each section of the hold were three or four latrine buckets. In most cases, a slave's shackles prevented him or her from getting access to the buckets.

During the Middle Passage, the slaves were brought on deck at eight in the morning and a long chain was run through their shackles and fastened to a ring bolt in the deck. They were then given tubs of pulped horse-beans, boiled yams and rice, and buckets of seawater to slake their thirst. During the day, they would be forced to exercise on the deck by dancing and singing. People were flogged if they moved sluggishly or sang laments. Women were often forced to dress in European clothes, decked with beads, and raped.

At four in the afternoon, the second mate and boatswain descended into the hold and supervised the stowing of slaves for the night, cramming tall individuals amidships and shorter ones near the bows to maximize the scarce space.

In bad weather, these routines would be suspended. Portholes and gratings were sealed against high seas and driving rain. In the hot, fetid holds, dysentery and typhus were rife. People lay in their vomit and feces, and European crew members would faint from the stench, dumping the tubs of food in the hold or not taking them below at all.

Lying in their own blood and mucus in a ship yawing and pitching in heavy seas, many slaves had their skin worn away until their shoulder bones, elbows, and hips were exposed. Crying out in fever for release from their agony, they would be brought on deck, swabbed down, and bandaged. Most died and were thrown overboard. In fact, of the sixty thousand slaves carried each year in English ships, nearly twenty thousand died at sea during the voyage across the Atlantic.

Many attempted to take their own lives. Some refused to eat and were flogged or tortured. Hot coals were held against their lips, or their mouths were forced open with a kind of caliper called the speculum oris. Some managed to jump overboard and drown. Others, like the "Muslims" in the Nazi death camps, simply withdrew into themselves and lost the will to live.

According to Walter Rodney, the Sierra Leone slave trade had been "prodigious," and he cites a slave captain called John Newton who made three voyages to Sierra Leone between 1750 and 1754 and filled the holds of several ships.

John Newton also wrote "Amazing Grace."

Amazing grace, how sweet the sound
That saved a wretch like me,
I once was lost, but now am found,
Was blind, but now I see.

Newton was employed in the slave trade for ten years, first as an ordinary seaman, then as ship's mate, and finally as master of two slave ships.

Like most of his contemporaries, he saw nothing wrong with the slave trade. "I never had the least scruple as to its lawfulness," he wrote in his memoirs. "I was upon the whole satisfied with it, as the appointment Providence had marked out for me.... It is, indeed, accounted a genteel employment."

His concern for his human cargos was no less mercenary than that of other slave captains. Quite simply, a dead slave turned no profit. This is why slaves who tried to starve themselves to death were forcibly fed, and those who jumped overboard were rescued from drowning. This is why slaves were washed, shaved, and sometimes rubbed with beeswax and oil, and why their wounds were bandaged. If their nails were trimmed, it was to prevent injury when they fought. If they were forced to dance, it was to keep them fit. If their mouths were rinsed with vinegar, it was to treat scurvy. If the holds were ventilated or fumigated with brimstone, if the decks were swabbed with disinfectant and holystoned, it was to stop the spread of deadly disease. And if lunar caustic was rubbed on yaws and a man with dysentery had his anus stoppered with oakum, this was to promote a quick sale in the scrambles of Kingston and Port Maria. Nothing was done for the slave because he was a human being.

Naturally, the slavers had God on their side. On one voyage, Newton inscribed the first page of his ship's log with a passage from Psalms 107: "They that go down to the sea in ships, that do business in great waters; These see the works of the Lord, and his wonders in the deep." Surviving terrible squalls off the coast of Sierra Leone, Newton praised the interposition of the Almighty in bringing his ship safely to port. When a slave uprising was put down on board *The African* in 1752, Newton perceived "the favour of Divine Providence," then neck-yolked the offenders and forced a confession from them with thumbscrews. Like other slave captains, he held religious services on Sundays, though not for the slaves. Indeed, Newton felt that captaining a slave ship was more favorable than any other calling "for promoting the Life of God in the Soul." In the evenings, when the watch was set and the slaves safely below "packed in their shelves," he would pace the deck murmuring his wife's name, recommending her to the care and protection of God, and composing such lines as these for the letter he would write her: "My heart goes often pit-a-pat, lest I should hear that you have been ill or uneasy."

He was, as another slave captain gibed, "a slave to one woman."

Undoubtedly, the pain of those he carried as cargo in his ships was construed as punishment for their benighted condition, not something for which he could be held accountable. As Veena Das writes, "Clothed in the language of responsibility, the discourse of power ends up with the equation that pain is equal to punishment and that the injustice of life, testified to by suffering, can only be redeemed by further suffering."[3]

In 1755, Newton left the sea and the slave trade and settled down to married life ashore. He was thirty. He wanted to begin anew. He made resolutions to get at least seven hours sleep a night, devote an hour a day to Bible study, avoid speaking ill of others, and forswear his past life as an "infidel and libertine." He began a diary with the words, "I dedicate unto Thee this clean unsully'd book and at the same renew my tender for a foul blotted corrupt heart."

But was it the slave trade he wanted to repudiate, or rather what he cryptically called "those brutish lusts by which I was once so long and deeply enslav'd"? Thirty-three years would pass before Newton lent his voice to the cause of Abolition, denouncing slavery as an iniquitous, cruel, and oppressive commerce "at which my heart now shudders." But was it God's "amazing grace" that brought about this change of heart or simply that he was sick of the company of rabble and unable to bear long periods separated from his young wife?

It is a dangerous illusion that we have been appointed on earth rather than improbably thrown into a world we did not choose and that no God oversees. Yet invoking God's will or Chaos can serve equally well in absolving us of responsibility for our actions. Slavery, inequality, and indifference to the suffering of others have all found their justifications in scripture, just as scripture has sometimes yielded the strongest arguments against these things. John Newton could conveniently undergo a change of heart without remorse since Providence had both approved his career as a slaver and brought that career to an end. And Brother Juniper, the Franciscan monk who wanted to know why God should have allowed innocent people to die when a rope bridge collapsed under their weight, avoided the question of why on earth no one had sought to ensure that the bridge was safely maintained.

About Time

Many of the most compelling experiences in life confound our expectations, elude our conceptual grasp, and are beyond belief. A "coincidence" is such an experience and "time"—its cousin-german—another. When René Descartes posited a rigid dualism between a purely spiritual mind and a purely mechanical, material body, he bequeathed to his successors—Nicolas Malebranche, Arnold Geulincx, and Géraud de Cordemay—the task of explaining how these separate entities could possibly work in synchrony. One solution went as follows: "what appears to be an interaction ('I move my hand') is a pure coincidence of two separate actions, each determined by the will of God." God determines that I desire to move my hand *and* that my hand moves. As for the "miracle of coincidence," Geulincx proposed an analogy with two clocks, each of which keeps perfect time. At the very instant the clock of mind points to the hour, the clock of matter strikes, as if a causal connection existed between them. But the connection is illusory. Mind is as enclosed within its own world as body is alone in its.[1]

Although the body-mind split may be illusory from an epistemological point of view, it remains experientially real, which is why, as Drew Leder explains, our bodies often feel absent to us in our everyday lives, as well as alien and beyond our control.[2] This phenomenological argument is crucial. It helps us acknowledge that while coincidences may be illusory or trivial for some people, they take on deep significance for others. The same is true of time. If measured by clocks and calendars, it is objectively constant. But everyone experiences the passage of time differently, depending on whether they are idle or overworked, old or young. Arguably, a hard and fast distinction between fact and fiction is equally difficult to draw since what one person calls verifiable may be, for another, entirely imagined.

There are certain writers with whom you feel an immediate yet inexplicable affinity. You have only to read a few lines to recognize, as if in another incarnation, your own inchoate thoughts put into words. This is how Gabe Linklater felt when he read the opening paragraphs of Thomas Wolfe's *Look Homeward, Angel.*

> A destiny that leads the English to the Dutch is strange enough, but one that leads from Epsom into Pennsylvania, and thence into the hills that shut in Altamont over the proud coral cry of the cock, and the soft stone smile of an angel, is touched by that dark miracle of chance which makes new magic in a dusty world.
>
> Each of us is all the sums he has not counted: subtract us into nakedness and night again, and you will see begin in Crete four thousand years ago the love that ended yesterday in Texas.
>
> The seed of our destruction will blossom in the desert, the alexin of our cure grows by a mountain rock, and our lives are haunted by a Georgia slattern, because a London cutpurse went unhung. Each moment is the fruit of forty thousand years. The minute-winning days, like flies, buzz home to death, and every moment is a window on all time.
>
> This is a moment:

He is eighteen. He bears the name of the angel Gabriel though has foresworn the evangelical faith of his parents. His father describes him as a disappointment, while his mother refers to him as her precious bane. He confides to his parents neither his ambition to write nor his impatience to leave home. Thomas Wolfe's writing inspires him to imagine another life awaiting him elsewhere, but like the invidious comparison between his own slight build and the gargantuan proportions of his hero, he fears that his faintheartedness will blight his dreams. At times, he tells himself that he has been steeped in his parents' biblical values for so long that the will to develop his own vision has drained out of him. He only knows what he does not want to be, so when he imagines his own future it is not drawn from within but purloined, like his image of Thomas Wolfe, from something he has read. It is not until his junior year in high school that he learns that the origins of his fragile sense of self can be traced to an event that occurred before he was even aware of his parents' worldview. His mother tells him about this event as a way of explaining his apostasy, shifting the need for forgiveness from herself to her son. Before he was conceived, she had been carrying a child who was stillborn. When Gabe was born a year later, she dressed him in the clothes she had bought for the child she had lost. Gabe grew up sensing he was a stranger to his parents yet unaware that in his mother's eyes he was the flawed replacement of another child, so idealized in death that the joy of life that found expression in him was, for his mother, a betrayal of his beloved brother's memory. Now he knows why he has always experienced himself as one of those colorless, celluloid negatives that fell out of his parents' photo album as he was leafing through it. A black hole where a star once blazed. It also dawns on him that his deep uncertainty about his own existence explains his susceptibility to superstition, and his search for coincidences from which he might divine his future. He knows that Altamont is the fictional name that Thomas Wolfe gave to his hometown of Asheville in the foothills of North Carolina's Great Smoky Mountains. He seizes on the uncanny similarity of the name of Ashe, Indiana, where he was born and raised, and Asheville, North Carolina, as an omen. In the summer of his senior year he boards a Greyhound bus and travels four hundred miles across Kentucky. In Asheville, he finds his way to the Old Kentucky Home in Market Street as if his journey across two states has been a journey through time and Julia Wolfe will offer him a one dollar bed for the night among her other boarders, and he will fall asleep, as his hero once did, hearing the mournful whistle of a freight train in the hills and dreaming of a northern city like an enchanted rock where he will be reborn.

Inauspiciously, the Thomas Wolfe House is closed for the day, and Gabe wanders through crowded streets, stopping from time to time to listen to buskers playing Dixieland jazz or Dust Bowl ballads. It is a balmy evening, with cafés and bars filled with tourists and the hubbub of voices. One hundred years ago, many of those who came to Asheville were looking to be cured by breathing the mountain air and bathing in the hot springs. *I lift up my eyes to the hills, from whence cometh my help.* It was his mother's mantra, though what help came to her he did not know, or to Thomas Wolfe who mourned the irreversible passage of time as he mourned the death of his brother Ben. *Oh lost, and by the wind grieved, ghost, come back again.*

He sleeps that night in a small park, his head cradled by the rucksack in which he had crammed two oranges, three salami sandwiches, a wind cheater, and *The Hills Beyond.*

In the morning he washes his face in the restroom at the Thomas Wolfe Memorial and eats one of his oranges before joining the first tour party of the day. It is a family from Boston. The two small children are bored and peevish and have to be repeatedly warned by the guide not to sit on any of the chairs or beds or disturb the place settings in the dining room. As for the parents, it soon becomes clear that they are under the misapprehension that they are touring the family home of Tom Wolfe, the journalist who wrote *The Right Stuff.* The father keeps asking the guide whether she has seen the film with Tom Cruise, and it is not until they are well into their tour that the exasperated guide finally tells him that lots of people confuse the two Wolfes.

"I told you this morning that it couldn't be him," the wife says, attempting to save face. "Why would there be a memorial for someone who is still alive?"

In his defense, the husband informs the guide that people often confuse him with Paul Newman, though his surname is spelled N. E. U. M. A. N. N. "There are two other Paul Neumann's, but few people know about them. I guess not a lot of people know about this Thomas Wolfe either," and he pauses before asking, "What did you say he wrote?"

Gabe is impressed by the guide's equanimity. She has a face like a porcelain doll. As she climbs the stairs to the second floor ahead of him, he covets her, and he wonders if her knowledge of the house and its history is evidence of a passion for Thomas Wolfe or she has simply rote-learned a few facts in order to pay her way through college. Yet when they enter the room in which Ben Wolfe died of pneumonia in 1918, the guide's voice falls to a whisper, as if the young man has departed this life only hours ago. "Some of the other guides read passages from *Look Homeward, Angel* at this point," she says. "They are some of the most moving parts of the novel, and Wolfe's descriptions of his brother's death are heartbreaking. But I don't like to do this. It makes me sad and casts a pall over the tour. So, when you are ready, we will move on."

Gabe wishes he could share his own feelings about those pages. Those moments when *present time fades*,[3] and you are haunted by a death you could not prevent and a presence that reappears in your life like a messenger whose message has been mislaid. But there is something forbiddingly circumspect about the guide, who clearly does not want to go off script. After hearing that many of Julia Wolfe's boarders had tuberculosis, and how few precautions she took to safeguard her children, the mother asks whether this negligence may have caused her son Tom to contract the disease from which he died, aged thirty-eight. The guide quickly assures them that there is no evidence that Tom caught tuberculosis during his years among the boarders, with never a room of his own, and with Julia so busy running the boardinghouse that he was often left in the care of his sister Mabel.

The next room contains a large double bed with a white counterpane. "This is where Tom slept when he returned to Asheville a famous writer no longer reviled by the locals whose flaws and foibles he had described in his books . . ."

"If he was as big as you said he was," the father exclaims, "how on earth did he fit in this bed?"

"I really don't know. It's a reminder that he was larger than life. Like Gulliver in Lilliput, you might say."

They are quickly ushered into a sunlit room that may have once been an open porch, where the guide recounts the story of Tom's infatuation with a young woman who occupied a nearby room. "One night, Tom climbed out onto the ledge that led to her bedroom, where he confessed his affections."

"Were they reciprocated?" the father wants to know.

"Love is always a mystery," the guide says. "Even puppy love."

At the end of the tour, Gabe is hopeful that he will be able to draw the guide into a more personal conversation, but after thanking them for their attention and wishing them a good day, she disappears into a staff room.

Gabe returns to Ashe to find that his application to the University of

North Caroline at Chapel Hill, where Wolfe studied, has been unsuccess-
ful, and he is obliged to accept his second choice of Indiana University
Bloomington. He shares a room in Eigenmann Hall with two other fresh-
men with whom he has been matched on the basis of "common interests."
Either a mistake has been made, or no other applicant shared his interests,
for he finds himself in a dorm room already decorated with IU pennants,
pinups, and flattened beer boxes. He suffers his roommates' drunken-
ness in silence, politely declining their invitations to parties and football
games. He spends his evenings reading in the university library, or at the
Runcible Spoon, trying to write. After attending a screening of *Breaking
Away*, he buys a secondhand bicycle and explores local stone quarries, one
of which is working overtime to cut new stone for the clock tower of the
IU Student Building, recently destroyed by fire. As he watches the stoners
at work, using old photographs and blueprints to reproduce the limestone
blocks of the old tower, he realizes why he cannot write. He does not want
to remember the past. Neither his father's hardware shop in Ashe, where
he worked after school five days a week, and all of Saturday, nor the nights
he knelt in prayer as his mother stood over him, unaware he was praying
for freedom from having to pray. He cannot recall if any reverie followed
her departure from the room, or whether, like Charles Swann falling
asleep as a child, images swept through his mind like sudden wind gusts,
and thoughts ran into a channel of their own, undistracted by the book
he had been reading, *the chain of the hours, the sequences of the years, or
the order of the heavenly hosts.*[4] If Proust and Wolfe switched between
being at the mercy of their memories and recalling every detail of the past
as a magical means of forestalling the future, he lives and longs for the
future, recording in his journal every new book he reads, every new class
he attends, every change of weather or season, even describing his roommates' inexhaustible delight in vertigo and obliteration, as if, unlike the
masons rebuilding the clock tower, stone by stone, he is building a new
life, word by word, from the ashes of the old.

He has been taught that there is nothing new under the sun. To see
every day as if from the threshold of eternity. To keep the Lord's day sacred,
to honor his father and mother, to bow his head in prayer, suffering adver-
sity in silence. At an Orientation event, he is invited to say a little about
himself, but the words die in his throat as if his father's hand is clamped to

his shoulder, calling him back to his duty before God. It will take him years to realize how deeply his father depended on him to inherit the business, preserve the family name, and care for his parents in their declining years. God might be there for them in Heaven, but on earth he is their refuge and strength, a very present help in trouble. Though they fear that university will feed the secular demons that have taken hold of their son, their greatest fear is that he does not love them and will never come home again.

His interest is captured by a course on the American novel in the twentieth century. He reads compulsively, mindful of both Thomas Wolfe's insatiable appetite and self-doubt. Indeed, he begins to wonder whether his hero's devouring passion was born of an unassuageable emptiness within him, a lack of love. It even occurs to Gabe that his boisterous roommates, with *their* constant binges and braggadocio, might be performing the same self-camouflage and are even more fearful of venturing out into the world alone than he is.

Whether Gabe's conjectures can be reconciled with the documented details of Thomas Wolfe's experiences in his first year at Chapel Hill is a moot point. Wolfe was often the butt of practical jokes. One night, as the six-foot-three Wolfe rose from saying his prayers and climbed into his iron-frame bed, the sabotaged bed collapsed under his weight, and his fraternity brothers rushed into the room to laugh at his embarrassment. Yet he would be remembered as a regular fellow, as genial as he was generous.[5]

It is not, however, glimpses into Wolfe's student days that fascinate Gabe but the recurring images of being alone in a country so immense and diverse that one's imagination cannot comprehend it. Lost in this wilderness, millions of human beings rush about, like so many ants from a disturbed nest. They race to catch trains and planes, forcing their way along thronged streets or subway platforms, feverishly working to meet a deadline or cope with all the demands being made on their time, yet never achieving the kind of peace of mind they might reasonably expect as the reward for their pains. It is then that the exhausted wayfarer looks back on a lost Eden, aware that it is impossible to return to whence he came, to the dreams that sustained him when he was young and first went out into the world, to seek, to find, and not to yield.

When Gabe reads Wolfe's contemporaries, he discerns a common motif: an anxiety about the future that feeds a nostalgia for the past. But if the past is to be recovered, the clocks whose hands move us inexorably forward must be stopped. Wolfe opens the floodgates of his mind to memory, and for as long as that image of the iron railing along the boardwalk in Atlantic City, or the "spoke-and-rumble of the ties below" a train as it crosses an iron bridge, is in his head, time hangs fire.[6] Jay Gatsby deludes himself that once he is rich he can turn back the clock and win the hand of the girl who refused him when he was poor. Charles Swann wonders how he can lapse into sleep or reverie, freeing himself from the succession of the days and the years and find a happiness that is outside time. Ernest Hemingway sees ecstatic love as the means "to have, and be, and live in, to possess now again for always, for that long sudden-ended always; making time stand still."[7] And when, in *The Sound and the Fury*, Quentin Compson's father gives him a watch that once belonged to his father, he hopes that it will help Quentin forget about time.

> Quentin, I give you the mausoleum of all hope and desire; it's rather excruciatingly apt that you will use it to gain the reductio ad absurdum of all human experience which can fit your individual needs no better than it fitted his or his father's. I give it to you not that you may remember time, but that you might forget it now and then for a moment and not spend all your breath trying to conquer it. Because no battle is ever won, he said. They are not even fought. The field only reveals to man his own folly and despair, and victory is an illusion of philosophers and fools.[8]

But the gift is a poison. It exacerbates Quentin's sense of being burdened by his history and cursed by his heritage, and when he tries to smash the watch in order to break time's hold over him it continues ticking even though it has lost its hands. The past is as unbearable as the future is impossible. Only by taking his own life on June 2, 1910, does he finally escape time.

Gabe wonders at the uncanny parallel between these passages in *The Sound and the Fury* (1929), and *Of Time and the River* (1935), when Ben gives a watch to his younger brother on his twelfth birthday with a warning to take care of it and not abuse it. When Ben asks his younger brother if he knows what a watch is for, and Eugene replies "To keep time with," it is suggested that the watch possesses the magical power to stay the passage of time, or bring the past back to life as in a dream.[9]

Gabe wants to interleave his own preoccupations with the ones he reads about. He knows what it is like to be crushed under the weight of the past. The God of Abraham. The sacrifice of Christ. The sins of the fathers, for which we must atone. He knows too that to feel free one must feel that one has a future that is not conditional on one's parentage or the past, and that to exist in time is not necessarily to be a slave to the ticking of a clock.

But what if the future looms before us as an apocalypse (as it does for his parents) or a catastrophe (as it does for those bearing the brunt of Operation Desert Storm). He can repudiate his church's vision of Armageddon or join protests against the Gulf War, but what can he affirm, what can he build on, where will he find his path?

His essay lacks coherence, but his professor is impressed by the questions he broaches, and the personal voice that finds expression in the academic prose. Gabe is encouraged to develop his ideas further. To consider a course in the Creative Writing program. And to read J. W. Dunne, who argues that, although a person is conscious of the world in which he lives, there is always another person who is conscious of that person, and another who is conscious of him, and so on ad infinitum. Accordingly, whatever one experiences implicates another's experience, whose time is not one's own. When Gabe reads Toni Morrison, he will instantly recognize this pattern of call and response, in which every theme is subject to recapitulation, as if time was contained within a small circle of people or group of jazz musicians, simultaneously echoing what has already occurred while voicing something that has not been heard before.[10]

It is late October. The time of windfall apples and yellowing leaves. A cold edge to the morning, as he cycles down country roads where the corn is withering, pumpkins stacked for sale, and flocks of birds filling the sudden sky like flung nets. He lies under an oak on campus, thinking of the girl he has been in love with for a month but never spoken to. He is agonizing over going home for Thanksgiving or finding some pretext to remain on campus. But he does go home, and his parents are pleased with his progress. It seems that hard work is itself a virtue and will be rewarded. He has already begun to write about his own life and has had glimmerings of the kind of writing this will be. Like Thomas Wolfe, and several writers he has yet to discover (Malcolm Lowry, Henry Miller, and James Baldwin), the writing and the writer's life will be as one. He will incorporate every detail of his life that can be remembered, and the work will only end with his demise. Moreover, the book will have neither plot (since life is random) nor dialogue (unless it is internal), nor characters (since the author is the main protagonist), and the drama of his inner life will take precedence over any drama unfolding in the world around him. Time, he has decided, is both viscerally and intellectually self-centered.

When he returns home for Christmas, his exams are behind him but not his anxiety over whether he has done enough to confirm the promise his teacher saw in him or the expectations of his parents. As he waits for his results, time drags, and the suspense becomes intolerable. Like Thomas Wolfe, his yearning for recognition is as deep as his fear of failure.

In the summer of 1935, Wolfe is in Berlin, anxiously waiting to hear how his recently published second novel, *Of Time and the River*, has been received. Similar anxieties had followed publication of *Look Homeward, Angel* in 1929 when, after furtively buying a newspaper at a Brooklyn kiosk in which the first review appeared, his superstitions immediately got the better of him. He did not read the review in the street but, hurrying home, "counted passing cars (an odd or even number decided whether the criticism was favorable or unfavorable)" and avoided "stepping on the lines between the paving stones for fear of bad luck."

"There was something comical and touching in the way [Wolfe] described his shyness of criticism," wrote his German publisher 18 years later, "and with that mighty fist that had nearly cost some Bavarian thickhead his life [At the Oktoberfest in Munich, Wolfe had got into a fight and thought he had killed a man], he furiously thumped on a little marble table in the Romanische Café, because critics in the United States had declared that he was just copying from life, and merely from his own life, at that."[11]

Gabe passes his exams with flying colors. At first, his father seems nonplussed. Unshaven in a collarless shirt, he snaps his braces then breaks into a broad smile as his son explains the academic transcript laid out on the table in front of them. Even his mother grudgingly admits that God works in mysterious ways.

His student loan for his second year is now secure, and he spends the summer working in his father's store. But a sea change is taking place in his ideas about writing, and his own future.

He no longer thinks of writing as an imitation of life. His dream of reviving interest in Thomas Wolfe is fading. He regards Wolfe's dependence on his editors to knock his work into shape as much of a flaw as his belief that one could still the onward rush of time by recalling and recording in exacting detail every event, every person, every place one has ever known. In his journal, Gabe writes, "You cannot transform the base metal of life into gold by alchemy or memory."

If I claim to have met Gabe Linklater when I was teaching at IU Bloomington in the early 1990s, and that he was a student in one of my classes, I would be both lying and telling the truth, for I have projected onto a young man I hardly knew aspects of myself that I have been reluctant to write about directly. As such, I have invented Gabe in the same way that Anthony Kerrigan and Alastair Reid (translators of the works of Jorge Luis Borges into English) conclude that there are as many Borgeses as there are readers or translators of him, and that, moreover, to read or translate Borges is to realize oneself in a new way.[12] The characters a writer creates are never sui generis. They are surrogates of himself, stunt doubles as it were, who perform tasks the author shies away from, unwilling to expose his frailty and flaws to the world. Like Geulincx's clocks, the author and his alter ego are, despite their separateness, mysteriously synchronized. They tick away in their own good time, and if they coincide it is not because God is coordinating them but because each has its origins in the same persona.

On the day I wrote these lines, I happened to bump into my colleague Charlie Hallisey in the mail room of Divinity Hall. When Charlie said he had been reading a biography of John Berger, I mentioned that Berger's *Pig Earth* had once made a profound impression on me, though I no longer read Berger with much interest. Charlie and I then conjured some of the authors that had spoken to us when we were young, including Herman Hesse, Lafcadio Hearn, and D. H. Lawrence, and we tried to think of any whose work had stood the test of time. It was a little like asking what aspects of ourselves had remained constant through the passing years and whether we would recognize, let alone identify with, our younger selves were we to re-encounter them. Charlie mentioned Yukio Mishima's tetralogy, *The Sea of Fertility*, in which each of the four books depicts what the hero comes to believe are successive reincarnations of his school friend

Kiyoaki Matsugae, who he repeatedly attempts to save from the early deaths to which his various iterations are karmically condemned. As an allegory of the twentieth century, the hero of Mishima's book, like the author himself, will fail to resurrect the lost glory of Imperial Japan and die like a samurai at his own hand. You cannot go home again.

March 15, 2019

When my wife asks me how my writing is going, I tell her it is perhaps going too well, because my fascination with synchronicity is leading me to see instances of it everywhere and even to recall coincidences in the past that I did not construe as significant at the time. In fact, I am being overwhelmed. Today, news broke of the murder of fifty-one worshippers in two Christchurch mosques by a self-styled white supremacist. Watching the news coverage, listening to those who had lost loved ones, seeing the New Zealand prime minister address the nation, and moved by the spontaneous haka that brought contending emotions of anger, grief, and solidarity to the surface, I found myself blinded by tears as well as mystified by the depth of my sorrow. Although I found it impossible to work, I was mindful of a passage I had recently read in Jung's introduction to Richard Wilhelm's translation of the *I Ching* where Jung speaks of "the coincidence of events in space and time as meaning something more than chance, namely, a peculiar interdependence of objective events among themselves as well as with the subjective (psychic) states of the observer or observers."[1] What subconscious preoccupations were welling up in me as I followed news of these violent events in my homeland? A particular configuration of yarrow sticks in I Ching divination or of stones in Kuranko divination enable a person to grasp thoughts and feelings that hitherto have lain beyond conscious reach, so what was pressing on my mind that I should react so personally to these events unfolding on the far side of the world?

To distract myself, I searched Netflix for a movie or documentary to watch. *Jane Fonda in Five Acts* would ordinarily have not been my choice. But today it was—as arbitrary as a fall of yarrow sticks or a constellation of stones on a diviner's mat.

In 1968, living in France, pregnant, and "attuned to be receptive to the ether, not just around me but in the world," Fonda is watching newsreel footage of the Tet Offensive in Vietnam and the violent police response to antiwar protesters in Chicago when suddenly she feels, "more than I ever had, American," and she realizes her country has "taken the wrong path and [that she] wanted to be with her people, in her country, to try to make things right."

Fonda had been introduced to the French actress and activist Simone Signoret by her husband, and she immediately sought out Signoret in her home south of Paris. Signoret opened the door, Fonda remembers, and said, "I have been waiting for you. I knew you would come to talk about the war."

I paused the video to take notes. I now knew who I was. My country was in me, though I was out of it, and I needed to be there, not here—in *its* landscapes, with its loneliness, its lostness, its history. It was all in me, and I was of it made.

That evening, my wife and I went for a long walk. I talked about going home. About it being time for me to go home. At one point I asked my wife why the temporal lobes of the brain were so called. "Has it anything to do with temporality, with time?"

"It's because they are near the temples. They're associated with language, visual memory, and the emotions."

Next day, I received a garbled email from one of my oldest and dearest friends, now in a rest home and suffering Alzheimer's. Ironically, the subject line of his email was *Memories*.

That night, my wife and I watched a movie called *Museum Hours* about a woman who travels from Canada to Vienna to visit a cousin who she has not seen since they were children. The cousin is in a coma and on hospital life support. Most of the film is about the visitor's chance relationship with a guard at the Kunsthistorisches Museum that houses, among other treasures, Bruegel's *Hunters in the Snow*. The film is very sad and beautiful. It is about the transience of life. Chance encounters. People who come together for a while then drift apart, lost in time.

Goethe borrowed a term from chemistry (*wahlverwandtschaft*) and made it a metaphor for the mystery of human bonds. Of such "elective affinities," in which one relationship seems to be preferred or chosen over another, the captain in chapter four of Goethe's novel remarks: "Those natures which, when they meet, quickly lay hold on and mutually affect one another we call affined. This affinity is sufficiently striking in the case of alkalis and acids which, although they are mutually antithetical, and perhaps precisely because they are so, most decidedly seek and embrace one another, modify one another, and together form a new substance." In response to the captain, Charlotte observes that "it is in just this way that truly meaningful friendships can arise among human beings: for antithetical qualities make possible a closer and more intimate union."[2] The term *elective affinities* may be extended to encompass all our relations with others—singular or collective, human or extrahuman—since in all such encounters we stand to lose *and* find ourselves; some aspects eclipsed, others thrown into relief. And since *something* transpires in the course of every encounter, leaving us slightly changed, human existence is always, to some extent, a living beyond ourselves. This is why emotions of anxiety *and* exhilaration arise in every interaction, and why face-to-face relations may be thought of as border situations par excellence, for here more than anywhere we risk confirmation or nullification and are made or unmade. We are thus, in a sense, all migrants. Every day and in every encounter, we cross the dark sea that lies between the known and the unknown, embarking on journeys in which we hazard all that we are and from which we return transformed. This is not primarily a struggle to find God or to come home, but a struggle for being itself, in which we are sustained by the faith that life will either be found or will find us. When tragedy befalls us, we sometimes say we are "undone" or "shattered," and "fall apart." We stretch our bodies, minds, or senses to the limit, so that we may escape the confines of ourselves. We still the mind and steady the body, altering our sense of who we are. We enter into relationships that change us utterly. We travel and see ourselves as if from afar.

PERSON TO PERSON

Confluences

In the summer of 1973–74, thanks to an initiative by my friend Michael Young who I had befriended at Cambridge two years before, I spent eight weeks in the Department of Anthropology in the Research School of Pacific Studies at the Australian National University. Derek Freeman, then head of the anthropology program, had brought together an exceptional group of anthropologists, including George Devereux, Meyer Fortes, Adam Kendon, and Peter Reynolds, whose research interests encompassed biological anthropology, human ethology, kinesics, and psychoanalysis. My conversations with these scholars enabled me to see, for the first time, how I might begin to fathom the mysteries of deep sociality—the sense of solidarity induced in neophytes as they undergo the ordeals of initiation, the spirit of *communitas* that comes of moving as one body in dance and to music, the rhythmic coordination of women pounding rice in a wooden pestle, the orchestration of gestures, the synchronization of bodies,[1] the harmonization of sound, the attunement of the senses, the marriage of true minds. In short, I was as interested in the possibility of overcoming *cultural* barriers and achieving an empathic ethnographic understanding of others as I was fascinated by those moments in everyday life when the line between ego and other becomes blurred, one's heart going out to someone in distress as if his or her situation were an imminent possibility for oneself.

It was Adam Kendon who introduced me to Ray Birdwhistle's research in the field of kinesics—the study of body motion communication. Using 16 mm film of everyday events—a children's birthday party, a couple flirting, two people greeting each other in a public space—Birdwhistle's microanalysis revealed choreographic, synchronous, reciprocal patterns of bodily movement that people were often quite unaware of. While psychoanalysis emphasized what people disclosed in speaking, Birdwhistle showed us what people revealed in their bodily interactions. As Fiona Macdonald notes, "When, before Breuer and Freud, if a man moved his leg up and down while he was talking to his wife, and an onlooker asked what the meaning of this leg movement could be, no one would have taken the question seriously. The movement was just something that happened."[2]

Painstaking analysis of filmed face-to-face interactions enabled Birdwhistle and his colleagues to not only parse movements far briefer than a leg bounce but to also show that such physical phenomena had the same affective and communicational force as speech.

At a memorable ANU seminar, I watched a 16 mm film shot at the birthday party of a child whose father was one of Birdwhistle's students. I was amazed by the synchrony and simultaneity of body movements between one individual and another. Because the time lapse of a single frame of the film could be precisely measured, it was possible to show that a coincidence of movements had indeed occurred. One could not, therefore, explain the synchrony in terms of stimulus and response or cause and effect.

Whether this was evidence of an acausal connecting principle, and how that principle might be described was not entirely clear to me. My initial reaction was to compare this behavioral synchrony to the mirror scene in *Duck Soup* in which Groucho Marx is unable to decide whether he is seeing himself in a "mirror" or someone else is imitating him in an adjoining room. But what came to intrigue me most was not the reciprocity of comportment or gesture, but the possibility that synchronic actions were expressions of the kind of intersubjective chemistry that Goethe spoke of as elective affinities.

It is not only between people that this chemistry exists.

When a BBC interviewer asked Magnum photographer Ian Berry to explain how he had come to take several of the most memorable photos of the twentieth century, Berry observed that one of the things he looked for was "the inter-play of gestures. You wait for things to come together. It all has to happen in a hundredth of a second, because frequently you don't have another chance."[3]

Love

Falling in love is perhaps the most remarkable example of coincidence that life has to offer, equal only perhaps to finding God. But the course of true love never runs smooth, regardless of whether the object of one's affections is a beloved person, a divinity, an admired writer, or a high ideal. Indeed, it may be that the best chance of preserving the ideal from the vicissitudes and vagaries of life is to keep one's distance from it, just as the mysteries of the heavens are protected by being light years away from us. It may be the same with unrequited love. Though it fills us with painful and unassuageable longing, it outlasts more worldly passions and figures, historically, in some of the greatest love stories ever told.

Some forty years ago, I heard a talk on NPR by A. Scott Berg, whose biography of the legendary American editor, Maxwell Perkins, was published in 1978. I knew a little about Max Perkins from my late adolescent love of the novels of Thomas Wolfe, whose gargantuan and untidy manuscript, "O Lost," landed on Perkins's desk in 1928. It had been Perkins's editorial skill and unshakeable belief in Wolfe's ill-disciplined genius that led to the manuscript's being pared down and radically reshaped as *Look Homeward, Angel*.

I was recently reminded of Scott Berg's talk. On a flight from Los Angeles to Sydney, I fell into conversation with a young woman who, for a year, had been in a virtual relationship with someone she'd met on the internet. She was now flying to Australia to meet him face to face for the first time and experiencing considerable trepidation. I never discovered whether things worked out for her, but her leap of faith set me to thinking about how our longing for love leads us to imagine its possibility even when we have no real knowledge of the one on whom our heart is set.

Something of this romantic hope informed the epistolary friendship between Maxwell Perkins and Elizabeth Lemmon—the relationship that Scott Berg had made the focus of his talk. In researching his biography, Berg had worked through a long list of names of individuals associated with Perkins, leaving the seemingly least significant until last. Among the barely mentioned names in the Perkins archive was the name of Elizabeth Lemmon, and when Berg traveled to Virginia to pay her a visit, he was convinced that his trip would be a waste of time.

In her youth, Elizabeth Lemmon had studied operatic singing, and in her old age she liked to listen to an opera in the afternoons. She invited her guest to join her. Though Berg politely sat through the opera, he had already lost interest in pressing this eighty-four-year-old woman to explain her relationship, if any, with the subject of his research. As he was preparing to leave, he was therefore surprised when his elderly hostess asked if he would be interested in seeing Max's letters. Elizabeth Lemmon then went to her bedroom and returned with a shoebox full of carefully preserved, chronologically ordered and neatly bundled letters. "These are Max's love letters to me," she told Berg. "I was Max's confidante," After a theatrical pause, she added, "Ours was a secret love."

Berg instantly realized that he had stumbled on a treasure, and that these letters revealed a dimension of Perkins's life of which he knew nothing. Elizabeth Lemmon would not allow Berg to take the letters away, though she invited him to visit her again, which he did several times, listening to an opera with her before spending several hours reading through the letters and taking notes for the biography he had, until this encounter, considered effectively finished.

There remained, however, the mystery of what kind of love affair it had been. The letters provided no clear answer, despite their deeply confessional character, and once again Berg was loath to ask Elizabeth a direct question.

Aware of what Berg was wondering but reluctant to broach, Elizabeth Lemmon took the initiative. One day, as Berg was leaving the house, she declared, "I never slept with Max. I never kissed him."

In fact, they met only rarely.

The first meeting was in April 1922. Max had been married to Louisa Saunders Perkins for twelve years, and they had five daughters. A devoted mother, Louisa also had a career as an actor/director and writer. This may have contributed to the growing distance between husband and wife, though the seeds of their incompatibility were probably there from the beginning, and only their shared Catholicism and devotion to their daughters sustained the marriage. Elizabeth was a close friend of Louisa's. Both were socialites who enjoyed financial security and had attended the best schools. But when Louisa introduced her husband to her friend, she realized that Max had not only been smitten by her beauty; he had fallen in love.

The pretext of Max's first letter to Elizabeth was an almost empty, cream-colored box of Turkish cigarettes that she had happened to leave behind.

Dear Miss Lemon—

When I found these cigarettes you had left I thought at first to keep them as a remembrance. But I am far from needing a remembrance. I then recalled that you had said you meant to stop smoking because cigarettes of this brand were no longer made & I thought I must save you from that dreadful heart-broken feeling you have when you don't smoke, at times, if only for the brief space these two cigarettes would last. If you have stopped, I feel as I have felt. This brief reprieve will make you think of me with extraordinary gratitude. Maybe that's too much to hope; but short of that, these cigarettes have given me a chance to say something too trivial to say without an excuse. It is, that I had just the faintest fear you might really think me so pusillanimous as to have been offended that you "could not bear the sight of me"—I guess not though. Next year, please remembe[r] I sent these & thank me. And I now thank you for all the pleasure you gave me—&, I suppose, everyone else in the neigh-bourhood—by being here this year[.]

> *Sincerely yours*
> *Maxwell E. Perkins*

I always greatly liked the phrase "dea incessu patuit."[1] But I never really knew its meaning till I saw you coming toward me through our hall the other night.

When one has been smitten, one is torn between a desire to confess one's feelings and a need to err on the side of caution lest one's feelings are unrequited, or come across as maudlin, inappropriate, or downright offensive. One writes to relate, but one is terrified that a careless word or clumsy gesture will destroy the bridge before a single step has been taken across it. Indeed, Perkins's adoration was less than fully reciprocated, and to protect himself as well as his marriage he ensured that his friendship with Elizabeth would be conducted at a safe distance, through letters. They wrote to each other for twenty-five years but avoided face-to-face meetings. In 1943, however, twenty-one years after their first exchange of letters, they met at the Ritz Bar in New York City. They sat at a small table and their talk touched on their relationship.

"Oh Elizabeth," Max said, reaching his hand toward hers, "it's hopeless." Elizabeth withdrew her hand. "I know," she said.

It was the last and only conversation on the subject they ever had.[2] In a letter she wrote him after returning home, she said, "I wish I could have seen you again while I was in New York, but the time was so short and so crowded."[3] The fact is that a prolonged meeting would have accomplished nothing. And everything points to the probability that there was no room in Elizabeth's life for love or marriage.

Before writing this story, I wrote to Scott Berg, telling him how moved I had been by his NPR talk and how it had stayed fresh in my mind for many years. But I had failed to locate a transcript of his talk, and there were details I remembered in it that were not in his biography of Perkins. Could he provide me with a copy of the talk?

Scott replied to my email immediately, saying that there was, to his knowledge, no published source for the talk because it was delivered without a text at the Edinburgh Festival, and that he invariably spoke from rough notes, as he did on that occasion, and unless somebody later transcribed it, there would be no printed account of the lecture. He then added that as far as he could tell I had remembered it remarkably well, better in fact than he had, and that I should rely on my memory and his biography to write whatever I wished.

It So Happened That...

So many life stories hinge on a single fateful encounter or remarkable coincidence that one is left wondering whether life actually unfolds in this way or human beings are compelled to discern design even when the evidence for it is imagined or circumstantial. I like to tell the story of when I first met the woman who would become my second wife, and we found ourselves one evening unable to recall the French word for spider. Perhaps we were blinded by love, for we simultaneously came up with the same wrong word—épingle, which means pin. The connection between *araignée* and *épingle* is as remote as the connection between spider and pin, but our love felt anything but arbitrary, and it was difficult to believe that our meeting had not been fated. Indeed, I went as far as calculating what we had been doing on a certain day in the past, as if it might be possible to find evidence that we were vaguely aware of each other long before we actually met, even though neither of us had any conscious knowledge of the other's existence.

When Jung speaks of synchronicity as an acausal connecting principle, I find this language too abstract, too impersonal. It suggests that meaning lies in a coincidence of events rather than a coalescence of lives. Just as most stories are about human relationships, particularly those that are emotionally intense or fraught, so too is synchronicity. It is as though our desire to find examples of synchronicity in our lives is born of a need to confirm that we are living the right life, with the right person, in the right job, in the right place. It is as if, lacking confidence in our own power to decide our destinies or know what is right for us, we are driven to seek some an external authority that will affirm our choices and approve our actions.

On a flight to La Guardia some years ago, I was seated next to a man in his late fifties. He fidgeted a lot, adjusting his overhead air vent, stowing his bag under the seat, straightening his jacket. At first his talk was fidgety too. Asking me if the temperature outside would mean ice on the wings. Talking about the American Airlines crash in northern Indiana the previous winter. Wondering why we weren't being served orange juice before takeoff. Once we were airborne, he relaxed, confessing that he had always thought of himself as a bit of a nomad, though this would be his first time in New York City.

"There's always got to be a first time," I said helpfully.

"You married?" he asked.

"Yes," I said, "How about you?"

"Like you said," he said, "there's always a first time for everything."

"You mean you're going to New York to get married?" I asked.

"You got it," he said. "First time in New York. First time married."

I was touched by his story. Now fifty-six, he had never been kissed. He put it down to always being a wanderer. Never long enough in any one place to meet anyone, to form any attachment. But it was different with Muriel.

"One day I had to go down to Brown County to pick up a reconditioned gear box for my Chevy truck. It wasn't far, wasn't a short trip neither. Well, I asked Muriel if she'd like to come along. You know, for the ride. Maybe have a coffee at Nashville. I knew she liked those dried flower arrangements they sell there. And I knew she didn't get out too much. She didn't say yes right away. But that evening she called me up. Yes, she said, she'd be happy to come. To keep me company. To see those dried flowers in Nashville. Anyway, we got the gear box and drove around Nashville, looking for a diner where we could get some coffee. I musta driven up and down that main street for twenty minutes. I was pretending to be looking for a parking space, but the truth was I was trying to pluck up courage to say something to Muriel, and I knew that if I stopped, if I wasn't behind the wheel of the truck, with my eyes on the road, I wouldn't get to say it. So we was driving up and down the street, not saying anything much. And then it was like something outside myself, like someone or something prompting me. And I kinda turned to Muriel and said those words that were coming into my head, just like that. I said, 'You're someone that it would be very easy to love.' I surprised myself. I guess I surprised her too. She'd never married. She'd been engaged to a guy when war broke out. When he came back from the war four years later she found out that he had been unfaithful. She couldn't reconcile infidelity with love, and so had given him back his ring. That's the way Muriel is. Never does anything by halves. But now she was hearing this word *love* from me, a word I'd never used before, that she'd probably never heard much neither. It was the same for her she told me later—like a voice outside herself, outside of us, was speaking. 'You're someone that it would be very easy to love, too,' she said. My very words. 'It,' she said. Not I. Isn't it strange that at the most intimate moment between two people, that moment of love, everything comes down to that totally impersonal word It. As though It, whatever it is, is doing all the talking for us, calling all the shots."

"Isn't that what love is?" I said. "Something more than us." And I thought of Georg Groddeck's essays on the It,[1] and of how, when two people fall in love, there is an overwhelming sense, not so much of a meeting of two separate human beings but of a mutual recognition that comes upon us with the force of a revelation or conversion, that our relationship has a life its own, and that we are being swept away in It, expressions of It, and that It has existed before us, and will in all likelihood outlast us.

Contrived Coincidences

In the course of my fieldwork in northeast Sierra Leone, I attended numerous storytelling sessions in Kuranko villages and recorded over 230 stories. Many of these were dilemma tales that hinged on bizarre coincidences that, it seemed to me, served as devices for creating ambiguity. By presenting an audience with a situation that confounded the normal order of things, people were inspired to reduce the ambiguity and resolve the contradiction, much as Victor Turner had argued in his study of Ndembu masks. "Much of the grotesqueness and monstrosity of liminal *sacra* may be seen to be aimed not so much as terrorizing or bemusing neophytes into submission or out of their wits as making them vividly and rapidly aware of what may be called the 'factors' of their culture."[1] The assumption here is that we are easily disconcerted by ambiguity and disorder, which call into question our taken-for-granted attitude toward the world. Images of chaos not only make us aware that order is to be preferred over disorder, but they also provoke us into actively restoring the world to right.

Keti Ferenke Koroma of Kondembaia was a master of the dilemma tale. He relished his role as provocateur as much as he insisted on respecting ancestral values. I visited him often to record stories and engage in deep discussions about the difficulties of resolving the tension between upholding moral ideals and satisfying personal desires, or sustaining a semblance of harmony in the face of competing passions and contingent events.

The following story begins as a story about three young sons of a paramount chief who set out on a journey from their natal village, hoping to make their fortunes and thereby not only find favor with their father but also eventually succeed him as chief. The three men arrive in a remote chiefdom where they are given hospitality. When the chief asks why they have journeyed so far from home, the first son says that he wishes to sleep with the chief's senior wife. "The morning after you can kill me," he says. The second son expresses a wish to sleep with the chief's eldest daughter, and also accepts death as the price for this favor. The third son asks the chief to kill his only cow, so that he can feast on the meat throughout the night. He too accepts death as the price of this favor. The chief agrees to these requests, but before daybreak the next day, his eldest daughter runs away with her lover. When the chief discovers this, he sends for the man who slept with his senior wife and cuts his throat. The same fate befalls the man who spent the night eating the beef.

Meanwhile, the surviving brother and the chief's daughter reach a great river. The crossing is guarded by a jinn who demands the life of a person as the price for allowing anyone to cross. On the other bank of the river, a woman and her daughter are waiting to cross the river. Captivated by the young man on the opposite bank, the woman says that if he agrees to marry her she will sacrifice her daughter to the jinn. The jinn accepts the sacrifice and divides the water so the people can cross.

The man now has two wives.

They reach a large town, where the chief has offered to give the hand of his eldest daughter in marriage to any man who can name which of his fifty magical medicines enabled him to become chief. Many men have guessed wrongly and lost their lives, but the chief's daughter takes a liking to the young stranger and offers to help him identify the medicine by changing into a tsetse fly and alighting on the one he should choose. The man makes his choice, marries the chief's daughter, and becomes chief in her father's stead.

Now the man's three wives fall pregnant on the same day and give birth to sons on the same day. The three sons grow up together and are initiated at the same time. Their father, the chief, lives for five more years, but following his death each of the sons claims the right to inherit the chieftaincy.

Now, which of the sons should be chief? What do you think?

[the dilemma arises from the rule of primogeniture, according to which the firstborn succeeds his father. But since all the sons were conceived and born on the same day, there appears to be no way of deciding among them]

Is it the son of the woman who saved the young man's life by fleeing her father's wrath before dawn? Or is it the son of the woman who sacrificed the life of her only daughter so that the man she had fallen for could cross the river? Or is it the son of the woman who betrayed the secret of her father's power to the young man? Of the three women, whose son do you think should be chief?

Now, before answering this question something needs to be explained. So listen to this story about Big Thing and Small Thing.

Big Thing and Small Thing had a quarrel. Small Thing claimed that he was the elder. Big Thing said that was nonsense. "I am the elder. Don't you know the meaning of the word 'big?'" They went to the chief. The chief told Small Thing not to be so impudent. He said, "Everyone calls Big Thing big and Small Thing small." But Small Thing said, "I am the elder, and if you follow me. I will show you why."

Everyone followed Small Thing from the village and on to the next village. Everywhere they went, people were quarreling, Small Thing urged everyone to listen closely and see what small things they were quarreling over. Small Thing would then say to Big Thing, "Have you heard that?" And they would go on to another place. At one place they came to, a great palaver had broken out concerning a man who had beaten his wife badly. Small Thing said, "Let us sit down and listen." Again, it was clear that the fight had arisen over a small thing. So Small Thing said to Big Thing, "People are always referring to me. Everything begins with a small thing." Big Thing could not deny this and accepted that Small Thing was the elder.

The people now summoned the son of the woman who betrayed her father's secrets and asked him why he should take his father's place. After listening to his claim, they summoned the man whose wife had sacrificed her daughter to the jinn and asked him the same question. He too made his claim to the chieftaincy. Finally, they summoned the man whose life was saved by the chief's eldest daughter. The man said, "I have very little to say. To everything there is a beginning. People should never be surprised at the way things end, but they should also consider the way things begin. My father went with his two brothers to a chief. My father's elder brother slept with the chief's wife. In the morning he was killed. The other brother ate the chief's only cow. In the morning he was killed. My father slept with the chief's eldest daughter, the woman who became my mother. Very early in the morning my mother advised him to run away. They fled. If my mother had not told him to flee, would he not have been killed? Therefore, since my mother was the first to save my father's life, every other fortune originated with my mother. Therefore, I should be chief. If a man is fortunate, he should never forget how his fortune began. My mother saved my father first, then the second wife saved him, then the third wife saved him. But they saved him only after my mother had saved him. If a person trips over a stone and falls down, he should not think of the place where he falls, he should think first of the place where he tripped. Therefore, all the fortune that my father enjoyed originated with my mother. Therefore, I should be chief."

Because of that argument, the son of the first wife, who was the first one to save the chief's life, became chief.

The problem treated in this narrative turns on the status ambiguity of the three sons. Because they were all conceived at the same time, born on the same day, and initiated together, the principle of birth-order position is nullified. Because succession is customarily based on primogeniture, there is no means of deciding unequivocally which son is the rightful heir. The ambiguity and confusion are reinforced by the apparent similarity of three crucial episodes in which three women saved the life of the protagonist in return for promises of marriage. In each case the promise was kept.

The ambiguity created in the narrative is finally resolved by the narrator himself. After considerable discussion, no one in Keti Ferenke's audience could judge which of the sons' claims should be recognized. Keti Ferenke approached the "trilemma" by shifting attention from the principle of birth-order position to the ethical dispositions of the mothers of the three sons. Even before these men were born, their fate was decided by decisions made by their parents.

At the beginning of the story, three men set out to seek their fortunes. Their fate does not reflect their status positions but their moral choices. The first son commits adultery with a chief's senior wife, the third is gluttonous, while the second elopes with, and subsequently marries, the chief's daughter—the least reprehensible of these three actions. In the second story, concerning the sons of the surviving brother, their fates reflect the moral choices their mothers make. The woman at the riverside kills her daughter, the third betrays her father's secret and so brings about his downfall, while the first woman's compassion saves her lover's life. Had it not been for her magnanimity, the young man would not have survived to encounter the women who became his second and third wives.

By confusing us with outlandish situations and violations of moral norms, Kuranko stories often deploy coincidence and ambiguity to startle us into seeing beyond the surface of events. For Keti Ferenke there was also a personal reason for emphasizing ethical judgment over social hierarchy, for he belonged to a marginalized branch of a ruling lineage, and in espousing the power of ethical intelligence (*hanki maiye*) he compensated himself for the lack of chiefly power. Insofar as his stories often involve a clever or ethically uncompromised individual deposing a corrupt or stupid chief, Keti Ferenke contrives the semblance of a fit between virtue and power. Elevated positions in the social hierarchy are thus made to coincide, so to speak, with moral dispositions.

The Double

It is no coincidence that so many stories resemble one another, variations on a finite number of universal leitmotifs. Jung refers to these motifs as "archetypes," such as the mother, the trickster, rebirth, and the shadow,[1] and Jungian-inspired scholars like Joseph Campbell's concept of "monomyths"[2] and Christopher Booker's model of "seven basic plots"[3] offer similar cross-cultural yet essentially reductive analyses of myths and folktales. One of these universal leitmotifs is the double. In no matter what culture or at what historical moment one encounters this motif, one is struck by the recurring idea that a person not only sees himself or herself through the eyes of another, but also that his or her very identity is an emergent property of intersubjectivity. In Oscar Wilde's story of Dorian Gray, a beautiful young man vows he will gladly "give everything" to remain young forever and have his self-portrait grow old in his stead. A "strange affinity" and "horrible sympathy" develops between Dorian Gray and his painting, and he becomes convinced that if his image dies, he too will perish. In the course of my fieldwork among the Kuranko, I sometimes heard of men who could assume the form of their totemic animal, though the shape-shifter risked death should a hunter kill the animal, unaware that it was a person. A similar belief is found among the Highland Maya. One's existence is mysteriously linked to an animal spirit—

one's nagual (lit. "disguise")—whose life runs parallel to one's own, so that if one's nagual weakens and dies, one also wastes away. In early Christian thought it was conjectured that salvation lay in the recognition of oneself as another, in the image of a divine counterpart wherein we glimpse what we might be or might become.[4]

Vladimir Nabokov regards coincidence "as a pimp and cardsharper in ordinary fiction but a marvelous artist in the patterns of fact recollected by a non-ordinary memoirist."[5] In making this distinction, Nabokov may have been thinking of his own treatment of the theme of the double. In his novel *Despair* (the title is an intentional pun), a man called Hermann Kanovich happens upon a vagrant who appears to be his doppelgänger though, ironically, the vagrant fails to see the resemblance, a fact that has fateful consequences for the protagonist, who seeks to kill his "double" in order to collect his own life insurance.

In all these cases, whether literary or ethnographic, there is some ambiguity about whether the double is actually another being or simply another side of one's own self. Perhaps, as in Hans Christian Andersen's ominous tale, it is one's shadow—a shadow that may displace one and act in one's stead. The theme is echoed in Fernando Pessoa's *Book of Disquiet*, where the author declares that he has "created various personalities within" and that in his dreams, these others become so real that he cannot be sure whether he is dreaming the other or the other is dreaming him.[6]

Pessoa's remarks put me in mind of Doug Wright's play, based on the life of a German transvestite, Charlotte von Mahlsdorf, who "lived openly as a cross-dresser under the twentieth century's two most conformist regimes—the Nazis and the Communists—for almost her entire life."[7] In parlaying Charlotte's life as a drama, Wright decided to present himself on stage "as her curator"[8] and not to shrink from the complexities of his character, who was a woman in a man's body, and her duplicity, for she was both a hero of queer history and a Stasi informant.

If there are two sides to every story, it is often because there are at least two sides to every human being. Sometimes, as with Wright's one-man show, it is possible to play out the inner drama of a multifaceted personality on stage. At other times, a narrative built around a series of external events is a more compelling vehicle for exploring the theme of coincidental identities.

Consider, for instance, the story of Gbeyekan ("Pure-speaking") Momori and his duplicitous namesake that Keti Ferenke Koroma recounted in the village of Kondembaia, northeast Sierra Leone, in March 1970.

At the beginning of the story, the two Momoris are close friends. Not only do they bear the same name, they also conscientiously share the profits from their collaborative endeavors. When it comes time for them to marry, they discover they have amassed only enough bridewealth for one wife. They therefore decide to share the same woman. When this arrangement proves untenable, the first friend, Gbeyekan Momori generously gives the woman to his namesake, declaring that if their trading is successful, they will soon have enough money to pay bridewealth for a second wife. But the second Momori schemes with his wife to kill Gbeyekan Momori and steal the money they have made. One day, traveling far from their village, they ambush Gbeyekan Momori, pin him to the ground, gouge out his eyes, and leave him for dead among some rocks. Despite being blinded, Gbeyekan Momori manages to drag himself into the shade of a great cotton tree where, it so happens, an old hyena and an old vulture meet each evening to share news of what they have seen and done during the day. Gbeyekan Momori overhears their conversation, in which the vulture confides to the hyena that it has laid a sixth egg in its nest, and that whoever breaks any of these eggs will have his wishes fulfilled. In turn, the hyena describes how, earlier that day, a young man was beaten and blinded beneath the tree and left to die. It is too bad that this young man is not here now, he says, because if he was, I could tell him that if he washed his eyes in the sap of this tree, he will recover his sight.

The following morning, as soon as the hyena and the vulture have gone on their way, *Pure-hearted* Momori takes a stone, dashes it against the tree, and washes his eyes with the sap that issues from the cut. He then climbs the tree and takes three of the vulture's eggs. After a long journey into an unfamiliar land, Gbeyekan Momori breaks one of the eggs and wishes for a large town to appear. He breaks the second egg and wishes to be made chief of the town. Breaking the third egg, he wishes to become the wealthiest man in that land. In the years that follow he marries many wives, has many children, and prospers.

As for the other Momori and his wife, they fall on hard times. Their luck runs out and their ventures fail. One day, hearing of a great chief who rules a distant town and possesses immense wealth, they decide to beg him for help. It takes them two days to reach the town and two more days before the chief grants them an audience. Despite their ragged clothes and woeful appearance, the chief thinks he recognizes the couple, and he gives them lodgings in the house next to his own and orders that they be fed and given new clothes.

That night, when the town is asleep, the chief goes to the house in which he has lodged his visitors. The man and his wife are afraid of the chief, and their fear only increases when he asks them to recount the story of their misfortunes. In telling their story, they pretend that Gbeyekan Momori died of natural causes. The chief then retells their story, describing what actually happened. Realizing the true identity of the chief, the man falls to the ground in terror. As he and his wife prostrate themselves before the chief and plead for forgiveness, Gbeyekan Momori says, I never showed you anything but goodwill. That is the nature of friendship. In giving goodwill you deserve to receive it in return. And so, tomorrow, I will divide my chiefdom into two. I will rule one half, and you will rule the other. We will share everything, just as we did in the past.

No sooner has the chief returned to his house than the man and his wife begin wondering how he became so wealthy in the first place, and as dawn breaks they go to his house and ask Gbeyekan Momori how he became so rich and powerful. When the chief tells them about the hyena and the vulture, they waste no time in going to the place where they ambushed and blinded Gbeyekan Momori so many years ago. The man finds the three remaining vulture's eggs and asks his wife what he should wish for. She tells him to use the first egg to get a large town in which to live. With the second egg, she says he should wish for a great river, since one cannot live without water. With the third egg, she says he should wish for her family to become wealthy, since a man with rich in-laws will want for nothing. What happens, however, is that the man's family becomes impoverished, and the woman's family take her away from him, and he is left with nothing.

The tale of the two Momoris brought me to ponder, perhaps for the first time in my life, the possibility that stories about significant others are symbolic explorations of divisions within ourselves. The duplicity and doubling in the Kuranko narrative make explicit the fault lines that lie within each and every one of us. Chameleon-like, we shapeshift from moment to moment, depending on who we are with, the situation in which we find ourselves, or the goal we are pursuing. The characters in our fictions, like the figures in our daydreams, are submerged aspects of ourselves, brought obliquely into the light. "Each of us is several, is many," wrote Fernando Pessoa. "In the vast colony of our being there are many species of people who think and feel in different ways."[9]

If this perspective means that I see the self as always implicating an other, it also changes my understanding of the creative process in which one makes oneself "into the character of a book, a life one reads."[10] Every situation we encounter, whether in fiction or in life, challenges the abstract terms we bring to bear on it. No matter how much faith we place in moral notions of the good, intellectual ideas of certainty, or social models of *communitas*, every situation in life, like every story, begins in doubt and seeks the conditions of existential viability anew.

Chinese Boxes

Stories often entail other stories, as if every experience is open to the possibility of alternative interpretations, none of which has primacy. Stories are not only embedded in life—in the biography of a storyteller and the epoch in which he or she lives; stories are often embedded in other stories. The *One Thousand and One Nights* exemplifies this tradition of frame narratives, examples of which can be found in ancient Persian, Arab, Indian, and African folklore. *The Manuscript Found in Saragossa*—written by a Polish aristocrat, Count Jan Potocki, in the first decade of the nineteenth century—is a modern masterpiece of this genre.

Potocki (1761–1815) was an adventurer, political activist, polymath, and pioneering ethnologist. Brought up in the Ukraine and in Switzerland, he spoke eight languages fluently, though chose to write in French. A real-life Munchausen, he served twice in the Polish army, fought pirates with the Knights of Malta, ascended in one of Europe's first hot-air balloons, and traveled the length and breadth of Europe and Asia, venturing as far afield as Mongolia and Morocco. His published accounts of his expeditions—including *Research on Sarmatia* (published in Warsaw 1789–92), *Historical and Geographical Fragments on Scythia, Sarmatia, and the Slavs* (published in Germany in 1796), and *Prehistory of the Peoples of Russia* (published in Petersburg in 1802)—contain considerable ethnographic, historical, and linguistic detail. Czeslaw Milosz calls Potocki "a precursor of Slavic archaeology,"[1] and Ian Maclean notes that Potocki's "published writings helped found the discipline of ethnology."[2]

At fifty-one, politically disillusioned and in poor health, Potocki retired to his castle at Uladowska in Podolia (now in the Ukraine) where he completed the *Manuscript* that he had begun many years earlier, inspired by his travels in Muslim Chechnya. In December 1815, he committed suicide. Legend has it that he fashioned a silver bullet from the knob of a tea pot or the handle of a sugar bowl given him by his mother, then had the bullet blessed by the chaplain of the castle before blowing his brains out in his library.

The *Manuscript* is set in 1739. A young Walloon officer, Alphonse van Worden, traveling to Madrid to join the Spanish army, takes a shortcut through the perilous marches of the Sierra Morena—a region where the influence of Europe succumbs to the Orient and Africa. Detained here for sixty-six days, he falls under the erotic and hallucinatory spell of gypsies, Muslims, and Jews, and listens to their stories. Over successive days, one story frames and entails another, until they come to resemble a set of Chinese boxes, or *matryoshka* dolls.

In 1964 a movie of *The Manuscript Found at Saragossa* was released in Europe. I saw the film in London the following year, though three decades would pass before I laid my hands on a translation of the book. In the film, the part of Alphonse van Worden is played by Zbigniew Cybulski, best known at that time for his role as the disillusioned nationalist militant in Andrzej Wajda's *Ashes and Diamonds* (1958). In the 1960s, Cybulski's tough yet sensitive features earned him the nickname "the James Dean of Poland." The first Polish superstar in the Hollywood tradition, a 1964 *Time* profile described him as having an unpronounceable name, "but women in a couple of dozen countries have developed a sudden passion for linguistics in order to fondle his exotic consonants."

Cybulski died on January 8, 1967 (coincidentally, my birthday is also January 8) at the age at forty, under mysterious circumstances. On the day he died, he had been due in Warsaw for a theatrical engagement. He reached the station at Wroclaw at 4:00 a.m., just as the Warsaw train was pulling out. He ran for the train and leaped from the platform onto a running board but missed his footing and fell under the train and was killed.

The accident may have been the result of fatigue or alcohol, but rumors spread that his death was premeditated. Unlike James Dean, who died at the height of his powers and glamor, Cybulski had become a paunchy, weary imitation of himself, giving lackluster performances under second-rate directors. Better to burn out than to fade away.

Quite apart from the fact that *The Saragossa Manuscript* has remained, for more than forty-five years, one of the most influential movies in my life, I have never ceased to be intrigued by the role that disenchantment and isolation seem to have played in the deaths of Potocki and Cybulski, and how these elements conspired with the wars and partitions that devastated Europe at the turn of the eighteenth century, and again in the mid-twentieth century, to lead both the author of the *Manuscript* and the man who starred in the movie to take their own lives. There are stories within stories here. Author within actor. The Orient within Europe. Europe within Africa. Nightmares within dreams. And, of course, ethnographer within fabulist. How can one endure such multiplicity and cope with such disparate origins and beliefs? And what creative possibilities might this fragmentation yield?

Here is another story, another ironic sequel to Cybulski's possible suicide. At the time of Cybulski's death, Andrzej Wajda had been contemplating making a film about the actor. Devastated by news of the death of his close friend, Wajda decided to go ahead with his plans but focus the film on the question of absence. *Everything for Sale* is also a film about filmmaking, in the same way, one might say, that the *Manuscript* is a story about storytelling. The film splices fiction and fact, just as the *Manuscript* fuses truth and illusion. Documentary footage of Cybulski's funeral and reminiscences by fans are included, and Cybulski's wife and many of Cybulski's friends figure in the film. Indeed, one of them—Cybulski's closest friend, Bogumil Kobiela (who would be killed in a car crash the following year)—walked off the set in protest at Wadja's opportunistic mixing of documentation and make believe. Wajda defended himself: "I used all the facts, events and anecdotes that I was aware of or which I witnessed during my many years of friendship with Zbigniew Cybulski. But I could never pretend to make a film of his life or about him in person. *Everything for Sale* will mostly be a film showing the impossibility of defining a man without his presence."[3]

The movie opens with an apparent recreation of Cybulski's death: a man is seen running to catch a departing train, then slips and falls and is dragged to his death beneath the wheels. Here we come full circle. If Potocki's *Manuscript* is made up of stories within stories, Wadja's film about the life and death of the actor who starred in the film of the book is made up of films within films. For no sooner has the man on the railway platform fallen under the train than the train grinds to a halt and an actor emerges from beneath the wheels to ask, "How was that?" It's a take in a film. But it's not the film's star who asks the question, but the film's director, who has had to stand in for the star who has not turned up on the set. Sometime later, searching for the missing actor, the director will hear a radio broadcast with news of the actor's death the previous night in a train accident remarkably similar to the one in the movie. The director rewrites his scenario. He now decides to make the star's absence a key element in the film, to create a movie around a person who never actually appears. Thus, Cybulski's actual death is reenacted again and again: by the director standing in for the missing actor on the film set, then by the actor, in reality, each replay dissolving further into nothingness.

A trail of footprints in the snow...

Henry James observed that for any writer "there is the story of one's hero, and then, thanks to the intimate connection of things, the story of one's story itself." It is possible to understand James's observation in two ways. First, no matter how remote from biographical truth a story seems to be, it is inevitably tied, obliquely and mysteriously, to the circumstances of its author's life. Second, just as every story implicates other stories, so the subject of every story implicates other subjects.

Stories are *about* the lives of individual subjects—persons living among other persons, subject to inner passions and compulsions, and under the sway of circumstances they can never completely comprehend or control. Stories are also authored and told *by* individual subjects—again, persons acting in relation to others, subject both to the influence of stories already told and the impinging pressures of their society and their situations. But the term *subject* has a third and abstract meaning, as when we speak of the subject matter or theme of a story. The term *subject* is thus "patently equivocal," for it refers simultaneously to particular *persons* as well as to universal attributes of human *thought*, including abstract, categorical, and logical generalities such as myth, culture, and nationality. As Theodor Adorno points out, it is fatuous to attempt to disentangle these two senses of the subject, for both the particular and the abstract connotations of the term "have reciprocal need of each other."[4] It therefore makes no sense to speak of individual lives without reference to the social and historical conditions that bear on them, nor to invoke universals without reference to the individuals who embody, experience, objectify, perpetuate, and struggle against them. In the case of Jan Potocki, his book is more than a picaresque about fantastic characters in a fantastic land; it encapsulates and allegorizes the disillusion felt by many Poles when the promise of the revolutionary era proved tragically empty. The bizarre interplay of dream and reality, reason and superstition, that permeates the fiction reflects not only the exotic range of Potocki's personal experience, it also suggests the terrible conflict in late eighteenth-century Poland between nationalist dreams and the reality of foreign domination. Though 100,000 Poles served in Napoleon's Grande Armée in the belief that Napoleon would guarantee the nation's liberation from Russian, Prussian, and Austrian rule, only 20,000 survived the retreat from Moscow in 1812. The Poles' last heroic stand was at Leipzig, on the banks of the Elster. Surrounded by Prussian and Russian forces, and wounded by three bullets, General Josef Poniatowski scorned surrender and spurred his horse into the river under furious sniper fire. It is tempting to see in Potocki's retreat from public life that same year, and in the book he completed in isolation before taking his own life three years later, a symbolic recapitulation of Poniatowski's heroic suicide and the melancholy culmination of dashed nationalist aspirations.

The Manuscript Found in Saragossa thus points in two directions—to the author's own itinerant life that blurred the borders between so many religious and cultural domains, and to the political life of the nation that surrounded him with its fire.

Autumn Leaves

We all carry significant others within us, and occasionally refer our actions to their ghostly and persistent presence—a parent from whom we sought but never received love, a friend whose praises we sang but never received praise from, a lover who died before her time. And our dreams of wiping the slate clean and starting afresh are often blighted by our histories.

In the heady days after Congolese independence in 1960, it was possible to believe that the colonial past could be erased, and one could start over. Certainly, Christophe Gbenye thought so when he ordered the execution of everyone who was literate or had worked for the Belgians. "We must destroy what existed before, we must start again at zero with an ignorant mass." Pol Pot decreed the same return to zero in Cambodia a generation later. As for me, I also thought I could leave my previous life behind, that going to Central Africa would be the remaking of me.

Nowadays, I am less interested in reincarnation than in those moments of intimacy when the gap between oneself and another seems to close. As when a piece of music abolishes time . . .

Often, the piece of music is banal and unworthy of the significance one attaches to the events it brings to mind. In *Tristes Tropiques* the French anthropologist Claude Lévi-Strauss recounts how, on the plateau of the western Mato Grosso in Brazil, he was haunted by a phrase from a Chopin étude. It wasn't that he had any feeling for Chopin; indeed, he regarded the étude as one of Chopin's tritest compositions.

The anthropologist is plagued by questions he cannot answer. Why am I here? Why do I press on, enduring this heat and hardship, this unpalatable food, this loneliness? He thinks of his colleagues in France, climbing the academic ladder or entering politics while he treks "across desert wastes in pursuit of a few pathetic human remnants."[1] He asks himself whether he is by temperament destined to be estranged from his own society. When he encounters a people as remote from his kind as it is possible to imagine, he finds himself overcome by nostalgia for his own past.

> What came to me were fleeting visions of the French countryside I had cut myself off from, or snatches of music and poetry which were the most conventional expressions of a culture which I must convince myself I had renounced, if I were not to belie the direction I had given to my life. On the plateau of the western Mato Grosso, I had been haunted for weeks, not by the things that lay all around me and that I would never see again, but by a hackneyed melody, weakened still further by the deficiencies of my memory—the melody of Chopin's Etude no. 3, opus 10, which, by a bitterly ironical twist of which I was well aware, now seemed to epitomise all I had left behind.[2]

Something similar happened to me in the Congo. In Léopoldville I spent much of my time writing a novel about my New Zealand childhood. When I finally returned to New Zealand, I spent much of my time trying to write about my experiences in the Congo or hatching schemes that would get me back to Africa. And a hackneyed melody was my link to that other world.

The melody was "Autumn Leaves." No matter who plays it or how it is played, I am instantly back in the Palace Hotel in Léopoldville where I shared a room for a while with a Swedish pilot.

Every morning Lars stood in front of the bathroom mirror in a clean white singlet, shaving with a blade razor. He managed to whistle while he was shaving, even with his mouth twisted and his chin thrust out. And it was always the same tune. At least it is in my memory. Once, when I asked him why he whistled the same damned tune every damned morning, he told me it reminded him of his girlfriend in Götland.

One day he walked out of the hotel after breakfast in his skyblue uniform, carrying his flying kit. He said he'd see me in a week's time. He was flying to Rwanda-Urundi. He was killed there, hacked to death with pangas in a refugee camp. What caused this tragic event was never established, though rumors were rife. After a few weeks no one spoke of him anymore. I had to pack up his things and take them to the UNRRA people at Le Royal. For a long time, I found it hard to sleep at night. I imagined him flying over the Mountains of the Moon to his appointment in Samara. I thought of his girlfriend in Götland grieving, perhaps playing "Autumn Leaves" over and over on her record player like the woman in the apartment I had occupied for a while in Parcembise, playing a maudlin song by Françoise Hardy. I found it hard to rid my mind of images of Tutsi warriors, dancing in splendid rows in the Hollywood movie of King Solomon's Mines—ostrich feather headdresses tossed to and fro, elbows jutting out, spears glinting in the sun, bare feet stamping the packed earth. The images of Africa you grow up with as a child die hard.

When I left the Congo, I tried to write about Lars and "Autumn Leaves." I failed. Years later I told the story to my friend Bill Maughan, who found a place for it in the book he was writing at the time, called *The British Empire for Two and Sixpence*. Every story in Bill's manuscript was prefixed with a postage stamp. He had found an old stamp from the Belgian Congo to head up my story. Except it was no longer my story. But I was happy that it had been told. An accidental memorial, perhaps, to Lars, whose fate could have been mine.

Magdalene of the Black Rose

On Easter Sunday, 1912, Frédéric Sauser found refuge in New York's Fifth Avenue Presbyterian Church. He was twenty-five years old and down-and-out. But Sauser's thoughts were less on his own destitution than on the plight of other refugees from Europe, "penned in, heaped up, like cattle, in poorhouses," or sitting in their shops under copper lamps, selling old clothes, books, arms, and stamps, or hanging out on street corners, vagrants, thieves, street singers, and panhandlers, all more in need of Christ's compassion than he was.[1] Moved by Joseph Hayden's *Creation*, which was playing, Sauser's reverie was interrupted every few minutes by a preacher making a sanctimonious appeal for cash, and Sauser left the church and trudged back, cold and hungry, to his digs on West Sixty-Seventh Street. After gnawing a hunk of dry bread and drinking a tumbler of water, he fell asleep, only to wake with a start and scribble down several lines that had come to him as in a dream. Falling asleep again, he woke a second time and wrote until dawn. He slept through the following day. At five o'clock on Easter Monday he took a look at what he had written and gave it the title *Les Pâques à New-York*. A few days later, he scraped together the $5.25 fare for a berth on a cattle boat to France, where he sent a manuscript copy of his poem to Apollinaire. Published that October, *Les Pâques* was celebrated as the first modernist poem, a clean break with the romantics and symbol-ists. Freddy signed it with his new name, Blaise Cendrars.

Seventy years later and six months after the death of my wife Pauline, I also found myself wanting to keep hold of the past even as I sought a new lease on life. It troubled me deeply that I could not conjure Pauline's image in my mind's eye, could no longer hear her voice, or feel her touch. At times I struggled against the silence and emptiness; at other times I submitted to it, not wanting to fill the void with my desperate longings, or the noise of my own grieving. And so I dreamed. Strange dreams in which Pauline would appear to me contorted and monstrous, dreams that were filled with disconnected words and images. Words I scribbled half asleep on scraps of paper by my bedside and typed up in the mornings after my daughter had left for school. These intense dreams lasted roughly ten nights, whereupon I worked on what I had been given, crafting a long poem whose central figure was Mary Magdalene, and whose leitmotif was a black rose. I had no idea whence many of these images had arisen, though my footnotes to the poem offer a glimpse of the constellation of elements that found expression in it.[2] Most remarkable, for me, was that the poem bore, both in its length and imagery, an uncanny resemblance to Cendrars's *Pâques à New York*, a poem also scribbled feverishly on the threshold between sleep and waking during a period of suffering and solitude.

Jorge Luis Borges has reminded us that a considerable body of litera-ture has had oneiric origins. Coleridge's eighteenth-century dream of Kublai Khan's thirteenth-century palace suggests eternal recurrences that operate on the souls of sleeping men and span continents and centuries. Rather than ascribe these recurrences to chance, Borges evokes the image of an archetype to which our unconscious perpetually and unpredictably returns.[3]

Is the figure of Mary Magdalene such an archetype?

For many years, Cendrars wanted to write a book about the life of Mary Magdalene. In *L'Homme foudroyé* (1945) he alludes to this work as a "secret book" on which he had been working for a year, isolated in his small apart-ment in Aix-en-Provence.[4] Titled *La carissima*, it was to be a fictional life of Mary Magdalene, "the lover of Jesus Christ, the only woman who made our saviour weep."[5] Though the book was never written, Cendrars would describe it as "the greatest love that has ever been lived on earth."

The same experiences that compelled Cendrars to write this book also demanded silence. "His silence was its truth," writes his daughter Miriam Cendrars. "Had he written it, it would have been, for him, a negation of this truth. Its truth is preserved in his silence."[6] One thinks of Wittgenstein, who fought in the same war as Cendrars, though on the other side. "Whereof one cannot speak thereof one must be silent."[7]

Magdalene of the Black Rose

à Blaise Cendrars

I

Magdalene of the black rose
I think of your voice
your willowy arms, green reach,
all of my days done with sudden rain;

5 Lady, into your hands I give
this stony body
these blunt words
this hail-hammered suffering hardened man.

II

On the Bridge of Sighs
10 I turn to your metaphors,
between a palace and a prison
come to you alone
Lady of snow and crocuses
who received me once in your white room
15 who made legible my life
who gave me ointments and fetishes
to brave my midlife passage
through this world.

You were the lamp
20 among entangled roots,
sure steading
on the steep descent,
you the bed of the river I crossed in flood;

I was the granary you filled.

III

25 Lady, I pray to you
 whose sepulchre is this blue sky
 its steps this hill
 whose frescos are of eucalypt

 I thirst for water
30 from your cupped hand
 I am the rosehip and persimmon
 I ask to be gathered
 from the gravid tree
 I want to be harvested.

IV

35 Ever I knew you in
 grass afire in Firawa

 Hearth-stones
 and the hunters' shrine,

 Saw you in cloud
40 at Waipatiki

 (all error I persuaded myself then)

 and that white bird
 of unblemished stone

 A lapidary crane
45 hatched from the sea

 That became a rumor
 of perfect womanhood . . .

V

 Memories of a theater, tar-
 paper pinholed with stars

50 A train thudding through,
 a man at the level-crossing gate

 Waiting in his car . . .

I enter the blue
flickering screen, the dark

55 Green hills,
having imagined for almost thirty years

I would find you
and recognize who you are.

VI

Full moon silvers
60 the river

I give myself over
to the thought we may be one

Lady of the dolorous
briar and tower

65 Here is your lover
saying you have abandoned him

Here is the adzed cross
of your son.

VII

Yesterday the sea was indigo
70 today the same
as the cobalt sky.

Lady, should I note these colors
seeing you in them,

Be led over stones,
75 my feet unsandaled,
and in you drown?

Do I trespass in your zone—
this heap of skulls
this rusted nail in wood
80 from which a cape of barkcloth hangs?

Are these your images
that stream in the sky

Claw at the cliff,
that twist like willows at the pool?

85 Do I visit this form on you—
breasts daubed with mud,

Blue whispers
accompanying me on the hill?

Can I trust myself in your arms,
90 my oppressor

My comforter,
feeling your breath . . .

Lady, are you indeed myself,
are you the sickness-unto-death?

VIII

95 Red ochres and yellow pigments
smudge my face. I am

In a darkening colonnade.
Lady, do I embrace

The myriad images, go down
100 through an olive grove

Toward the sea, come
at evening to a village

Whose ikon is a snake, meet
that dancer

105 Braceleted with bone
whose voice is pitched

On the rising wind?

The thought of your body
keeps me from sleep,

110 I yearn
for the music of flutes

I heard in Firawa
above the rain.

IX

When my lover died
115 they dismembered and burned her

Strewing the river
with her ash,

And for a year
I traced its source to the mountains,

120 Descended it to the sea
singing her name

Seeking the understanding she had lived.

And then in the dry season
you in the shape of birds

125 Answered as I sang. You drew the ash
from crocodile and fish

Sieved it from sand,
refashioning her who had become for me

The river,
130 her voice the cataract,

And my arms branched again
and bore green foliage

And the rains came
and my body was a bridge

135 On which you walked
into a hinterland
of promises

Lady,
and I gave you all I had to give.

X

140 The river relinquishes
hills wholly still as their cuneiform

Shadows rise
out of the valley.

I open my heart to them
145 that have destroyed
everything I know I am.

Night lifts itself
from the valley floor—

One mountain thrown
150 against its opposite—

Your life and mine,
the daylight going, needful

Of the dark,
and the broadcast stars—

155 Orion, Betelgeuse—
salt-rimed names a sailor gave

To the mountains here:
Stargazer, Moonraker, Tantalus,

Until we are no more
160 than what appears of us

In wind-combed grasses
under a glacier.

XI

That which moved like the wind
and was sown like stars

165 No more a property of moving
than was foliage or cloud

Than these words are...

It is some other uses me,
giving and taking despite my will

170 Determining the furrow
of the turning plough.

My mind is clouded. Images
sift through me like earth.

I lie under the cordylines again
175 at Maungahania

Hearing the wind
in which I was quieted.

XII

Alive to you again
I remember circling frigate birds

180 At a feast of death and resurrection,
heads of a blue harbour

Bruised by rain.
Now to the day

Seaward and landward
185 you return

Who lay with me all winter
in rock and pine

Always you, mistress of my silences,
telling me what to say.

XIII

190 Over a besieged city
you threw the folds of your blue gown.

When soldiers stole your icon
their sledges would not move

In the heavy snow

195 They slashed your face;
your scars weep when we suffer now.

So the suffering in our lives repeats
events 300 years ago . . .

A dark island among wheat
200 the blond moonlight and someone dying

The dark islands of ourselves
waiting for miracles

Kneeling on stone flags
gazing at your face

205 Madonna of the rock
that was not taken,

Survivor of the nightlong pillaging

Guardian of the street
savior of this penitent

210 Magdalene of the black rose.

NOTES TO POEM

Line 9   The Bridge of Sighs in Venice connected the Doge Palace and the state
prisons; over it condemned prisoners were led from the judgment hall
to the place of execution. Lines 13–16, however, allude to memories of
the Bridge of Sighs over the Cam at St. John's College, Cambridge.

11   Cf. Byron: Childe Harold's Pilgrimage, iv, I.

26–28   Mt. Taylor, Canberra.

36   Firawa: a Kuranko village in northeast Sierra Leone.

40   Waipatiki (lit. "flounder water"): a place on New Zealand's Wairarapa
coast where Pauline and I sometimes spent weekends. Allusions are
also made to James K. Baxter's poem "Waipatiki Beach" in Pig Island
Letters (1966).

42–47   Ambukur is a stone representing perfect womanhood—the focus of a
male cult among the Gamagai, West Highlands, Papua New Guinea.
My closest Canberra friends at the time I wrote this poem—Kathy Gol-
ski and Woijcieck Dabrowki—have kindly forgiven the liberties my
unconscious has taken with the stories they told me of Ambukur.

48–54   References are made to Machaty's silent film, Ecstasy, starring Hedy
Lamarr.

64   Briar and tower: The Sleeping Beauty and Rapunzel—figures confined
in time and space respectively.

67–68   According to certain medieval allegories, the Virgin Mary is not only
the mother of Christ but also his cross.

77–86   Kali. Jung notes that in Sankhya philosophy the mother archetype is
elaborated into the concept of prakrti (matter), with three fundamental
attributes or gunas assigned to it: goodness, passion, and darkness.

114–137 An oneiric adaptation of a Kuranko narrative, "The Story of Na Nyale,"
published in my Allegories of the Wilderness: Ethics and Ambiguity in

Kuranko Narratives (Bloomington: Indiana University Press, 1982), 203–8.

146–162 These images are of the Matukituki Valley in Mt. Aspiring National Park, New Zealand, where Pauline and I spent a memorable summer with our friends Bryn and Isabelle Jones. Elements of James K. Baxter's "Poem in the Matukituki Valley" are also alluded to.

170–171 An etymological link exists between the action of the plowman turning at the end of each furrow and the poet turning at the end of each line: versus/verse.

174–176 Maungahania is a marae overlooking the Waiapu River on the east coast of New Zealand. The source of the image of the wind (te hau) is a summer day that Pauline and I were sitting with Te Pakaka Tawhai and Henare Ngata on the porch of the "bungalow" at Waiomatatini and were suddenly overwhelmed by a warm wind moving across the river flats toward us, shaking the leaves of the cabbage trees.

190–198 The allusions are to the Black Madonna of Czestochowa in Poland, and to the siege of the monastery of Czestochowa by the Swedish army in 1648 during the Thirty Years' War.

All the Birds of the Air

When Pauline died, my daughter and I left New Zealand in the hope of making a fresh start in Australia. But even as new landscapes and new friends brought me back to life, my shattered soul drew me downward as if like Orpheus, having lost my Eurydice, I could no longer bear the light of day. There were times, therefore, when the boundary between the world around me and the world within became so blurred that I was alienated from both. Alone in the house one afternoon, I took a break from the memoir I was writing about the eighteen years of my marriage and went into the kitchen to brew a cup of tea. I immediately became aware of an agitated bird outside the kitchen window. Fluttering against the pane, it gave the impression of wanting to get into the house. Rebuffed by the glass it would flutter away before returning moments later, hurling itself against the window as if trying to break through. I became convinced that the bird embodied the spirit of my late wife, and that it was desperately seeking reunion with me. It was, I later thought, as if my own fluttering heart had found in the bird's desperate movements an analogue of my own searching. But such coincidences involve many elements, and I can now see the multiple strands that became woven into that one moment in time.

As a solitary child I developed a preternatural relationship with pine plantations, rock formations, hills and rivers. They were, for me, imaginary friends, so when my wife died, I sought and found solace in the rocks and grass on the mountain near my Canberra house, and I imagined that my wife's spirit had found a home there. My response to the bird at my window, however, had a more specific source, for when I was doing fieldwork in a remote village in northern Sierra Leone, and often separated from Pauline, who was pregnant at the time, I sometimes succumbed to anxieties about her well-being. One evening during my first extended stay in Firawa, I went out to a latrine in the grassland behind my house. Within minutes, I was surrounded by a flock of Senegalese firefinches (*tintingburuwe*). These small crimson birds nested in the eaves of houses and scavenged like sparrows on husks of grain and food scraps. Because of their close association with the rubbish heaps (*sundukunyema*) where children who die before weaning are often buried, it is understandable that Kuranko women should imagine that the souls of their dead infants find a temporary home in the birds. At the sight of these clamoring birds, it was almost inevitable that I would be overwhelmed by sudden panic, thinking that Pauline had suffered a miscarriage, and that I should return to Kabala. Instead, I consulted a diviner and let myself be assured that she was all right, and so I stayed on in the village until the cycle of events associated with the initiation of girls had been completed.

Jung might see in my conflation of Pauline and the bird at my window evidence of the collective unconscious. Indeed, he writes of a patient of his who described how, "at the deaths of her mother and her grandmother, a number of birds gathered outside the windows of the death-chamber," and later, when her husband fell gravely ill, "a whole flock of birds alighted in their house, reminding her of what had happened as her mother and grandmother lay dying."[1] In this case and mine, the association of birds with angels who wing their way between earth and ether, bearing messages from God, was a cultural given, but when Jung claims that "it is not too far-fetched to suppose that there may be some archetypal symbolism at work," and goes on to evoke Babylonian images of the souls of the dead wearing feathered headdresses and Egyptian notions of the souls of the dead as birds, I cannot follow him. For, in my case at least, it was possible to identify a number of far more immediate elements that my subconscious could seize on in its desperate attempt to objectify, and externalize and ultimately manage, my inner disquiet.

PLACE TO PLACE

The Relativity of Our Viewpoints

I suspect that we are intrigued by coincidences for the same reason that we are amused by puns. Synchronous events, like plays on words, reveal unexpected meanings and inspire good stories. We might, however, spare a thought for unhappy coincidences when meaning is lost or cannot be found.

In the autumn of 1922, Ernest Hemingway was living in Paris and working as a correspondent for the *Toronto Star*. That November, he was dispatched to Switzerland to cover the Peace Conference in Geneva. Missing his wife Hadley, who had remained in Paris nursing a cold, Hemingway wrote to her, urging that she join him and that, as soon as the conference was over, they go sightseeing in the mountains. When packing for the trip, Hadley decided to bring Hemingway's manuscripts with her, including the short stories he had been working on in Paris.

At the Gare de Lyon, she boarded her train and stowed her bags in the overhead rack. She then left the train to buy some water. When she returned to her compartment, the small overnight bag in which she had packed her husband's manuscripts had disappeared. Despite searching the train with the conductor, the missing suitcase could not be found, and Hadley had to return to her seat and wonder how she was going to break the news to Hemingway when she met him in Lausanne, and how he would react.

Recalling this episode forty years later, Hemingway wrote, "I had never seen anyone hurt by a thing other than death or unbearable suffering except Hadley when she told me about the things being gone. She had cried and cried and could not tell me. I told her that no matter what the dreadful thing was that had happened nothing could be that bad, and whatever it was, it was all right and not to worry. We could work it out. Then, finally, she told me. I was sure she could not have brought the carbons too ..."[1]

Hemingway's stoic attitude is admirable. He says he had learned never to discuss casualties. Besides, it was probably not a bad thing to have lost his early work, and he would write more stories. But he admits to saying these things to his wife and friends to alleviate *their* distress by giving the impression that he had not been devastated by the mishap.

Hemingway would connect this loss to his iceberg theory of writing, according to which the deeper meaning of a story is never evident on the surface. In *The Moveable Feast* he remembers a story he called "Out of Season" and his decision to omit the original ending in which the old man hangs himself. You can omit almost anything, he would say, and "the omitted part would strengthen the story and make people feel something more than they understood."[2]

Hadley's divorce from Hemingway in 1927 was probably not connected to the loss of his manuscripts, but did the things he omitted from his memoir of his Paris years strengthen his image?

"We live ... lives based upon selected fictions," Lawrence Durrell has Pursewarden say in the second volume of his almost forgotten *Alexandria Quartet*. "Our view of reality is conditioned by our position in space and time—not by our personalities as we like to think."[3]

During the years that Hemingway and Hadley lived in Paris (1921–26) Hemingway encountered the pioneering modernist poet Blaise Cendrars.

Thirty years later, Hemingway recalls the encounter in *A Moveable Feast*:

> The Closerie des Lilas had once been a café where poets met more or less regularly and the last principal poet had been Paul Fort whom I had never read. But the only poet I ever saw there was Blaise Cendrars, with his broken

boxer's face and his pinned-up empty sleeve, rolling a cigarette with his one good hand. He was a good companion until he drank too much and, at that time, when he was lying, he was more interesting than many men telling a story truly. But he was the only poet who came to the Lilas then and I only saw him there once.[4]

A page later, Hemingway's pettiness gets the better of him. After describing some of the veterans who used to frequent the Lilas, he says that in those days one did not trust anyone who had not been in the war . . . "and there was," he adds, "a strong feeling that Cendrars might well be a little less flashy about his vanished arm."

Here is Cendrars's more generous recollection of the same occasion:

> I was drinking; he was drinking at a table next to mine. He was with an American sailor on leave. He was in uniform—probably that of a non-combatant ambulance aide, unless I'm mistaken. I had already lost my arm. It was the end of that other war, the last of the last. We talked between tables. Drunks love to talk. We talked. We drank. We drank again. I had an appointment in Montmartre with the widow of André Dupont, a poet killed at Verdun. I went there every Friday to eat bouillabaisse with Satie, Georges Auric, Paul Lombard, and, sometimes, Max Jacob. I brought my boozer American friends with me, thinking I'd give them something good *de chez nous* to eat. But the Americans aren't fond of good food; they have no good food at home; they don't know what it is. Hemingway and his sailor didn't care for my arguments. They preferred to drink until they weren't thirsty any more. So I planted them in a bar on the rue des Martyrs, I can't remember which, and ran to treat myself at my friend's widow's house.

Henry Miller saw nothing but envy in Hemingway's recollections. Cendrars was the authentic man of the world, the *bourlinguer* that Hemingway dreamed of becoming, and Miller made no bones about it. Hemingway was "a phony, a gutless coward compelled by weak nerves to turn to violence, the way others turn to drugs or madness." Miller hated Hemingway's "two-fisted, bravado brawling side, the pose of the *aficionado*—hunter of wild beasts, fisher of sharks, bandoliered soldier heading into battle." According to Miller, Hemingway was nothing more than a bully, bolstered by media myths, and he felt no scrap of admiration for Hemingway's "stenographic" style, in which reality is "traced by the eye alone in the absence of the brain."[5]

Perhaps Simenon should be allowed to have the last say.

When Hemingway died, five months after Cendrars, several obituary writers spoke of the two authors in the same breath—both larger than life, legendary in their ability to mix worldliness with literature. Simenon dismisses the comparison. A parallel might be drawn between their lives, he says, but their deaths were utterly different.

While Hemingway chose to commit suicide rather than endure a painful and lingering death, Cendrars took exactly the opposite course of action.

> Far from killing himself, he lived with his illness for many years, paralysed, fighting it tooth and nail, and, I'm told, refusing to take any of the medicines that would have eased his suffering, so that, despite everything, he would keep his lucidity. I believe this. This was just like him. For I knew him well.[6]

We all reflect so differently on one another that it is impossible to know where *the truth* lies. But one can, I think, evaluate our actions and ideas in relation to life, asking whether we increase or diminish it in the ways we choose to write about it. By life I do not mean just *my* life or *yours*, but life with a capital *L*, encompassing all that surrounds and outlasts us, and which we variously call history, nature, God, or tradition. I like to think of this encompassing environment as the sea, so that when one stands on some shoreline and thinks to oneself, this is the same sea Sophocles described, the same tides that washed the pebbles on Dover Beach... the clouds rolling, dispersing, bundled across the sky by the wind, these are the same clouds that Virginia Woolf saw on that spring day when she walked around Oxford, taking notes for her *Room of One's Own*.

As Time Goes By

Umberto Eco observes that imperfect stories are sometimes more compelling than perfect ones, and that the reason Ingrid Bergman seems so mysterious in *Casablanca* is because, when the film was being shot, no one knew until the last moment whether Ilse would leave with Rick or Victor. Ingrid Bergman simply "did not know at which man she was to look with greater tenderness," which is "why, in the story, she does not, in fact, choose her fate: She is Chosen."[1]

When I met Renata, she did not look like Ingrid Bergman, but she behaved like her. She didn't seem to know at which man she was to look with greater tenderness either.

For five weeks—as long as it took for the *Fairstar* to sail from Melbourne to Genoa—she kept me waiting and wondering. All that time I thought Mario was waiting and wondering too, though when Renata went off with him at the end of the voyage, I consoled myself that it had been inevitable all along.

She was tall, with dark cropped hair. And she possessed that air of mysterious sadness that made Ingrid Bergman's performance in *Casablanca* so memorable. Her children clung to her, pressing their faces into her skirt when you tried to talk to them. The little boy was about five, his sister a year or so younger. When they buried their faces in their mother's skirt, she would place her hands on their heads and look questioningly at the person who had dared address them. So men learned to wait until she was alone, sunning herself by the pool or sitting at the bar before dinner. One by one they would approach her with offers to buy her a drink, invitations to deck games, sometimes direct propositions. We would observe her pained expression, the brusque gesture toward the door that suggested she would soon have to go to the children. Then we would watch with satisfaction as the suitor sidled back to his table looking for all the world as if he'd been accused of child molestation. Yet she would sit in her deck chair by the swimming pool, rubbing sun cream into the children's shoulders, and gaze darkly at us all, aloof and beautiful, as if it was only a matter of time before she chose one of us as her lover.

I was foolish enough to think it was a choice between Mario and me. Mario devoted more attention to her than anyone, buying candies and board games for her children, asking if she would do him the honor of allowing him to escort her to the dance, proposing breathtaking excursions at our next port of call. I pretended to have no designs on her at all. Later, when she told me that she had been completely taken in by my apparent indifference, I was amazed. I had assumed that my infatuation was embarrassingly obvious.

The truth was we were both far from her thoughts. When she sauntered barefoot around the boat deck in a sarong and bikini top and we tried to outplay each other at the tenniquoits net she was agonizing about the decision she had made to return to Italy with the children, ostensibly so they could spend some time with their grandparents, but possibly because Renata was hoping that, in the event of a divorce, her Australian husband would not sue for custody of the children. When she stood at the taffrail in the dusk, staring at the ship's wake or some unidentified Indonesian island, she was wondering whether her parents in Pinzolo would have room to accommodate her and the children, whether they would lecture her on her duties as a wife and mother, wearing her down with talk of the shame she had brought on them and the village until she would one day leave and go back to the man she had married against their wishes. She was hoping the voyage would never end, that the ship would sail forever from one tropical port to another until her course became clear. But she knew that time was against her, and that between a dilapidated bungalow in Fitzroy and a cramped farmhouse in the Trentino-Alto Adige there was pitch darkness.

The first time I talked to Renata we were in the ship's library. She was borrowing Katherine Mansfield's journals. I told her I was a New Zealander. She smiled, as though I'd intended some kind of joke. She asked me what I was reading. I had a paperback edition of Van Gogh's letters in my hand. She asked if she could borrow it after me. I said I would swap it for the Katherine Mansfield.

When I began reading Vincent's letters, I took notes, anticipating the time when Renata would read them too and we would share our reflections.

One letter in particular made a deep impression on me. It helped me begin to understand what had gone wrong for me in Australia where I had worked in Aboriginal welfare. Vincent wrote it to Theo in the winter of 1880, after a period of estrangement between the brothers, and confides that his "only anxiety is: how can I be of use in the world?" At the time, he is preparing to be an evangelist among the coal miners of the Borinage region, west of Mons. In order to commit himself body and soul to the poor, he feels he must cut himself off from his family, to "cease to exist" for them. He neglects his appearance, goes hungry and cold, and gives the little he has to peasants and workers. But who is helped by this self-abasing sympathy? What good can come of this identification with the oppressed? Vincent feels imprisoned and melancholic. Thwarted in his efforts to alleviate the misery of humankind, he ends up seeking to annihilate his anguish by immersing himself in the suffering around him. But no one is helped by this, nothing is really changed. In this act of martyrdom, the martyr has simply made his guilt disappear by a sleight of hand, donning the sackcloth of those he had set out to save.

When Renata asked me what I thought of Van Gogh's letters, I told her I was intrigued by the way Vincent's zeal to improve the lot of the peasants and miners was gradually eclipsed by a desire to paint peasant life. And I ventured to say that I too was wrestling with the dilemma of whether to pursue a life as an activist or artist.

"But there are many ways of being responsive to the world around us," Renata said. "I love it when Katherine Mansfield talks of passing an apple stall and becoming so entranced by the apples that she changes into an apple! I love it when she describes herself writing so sympathetically about ducks that she feels herself turning into a duck. I think that's a wonderful experience to have, even if it doesn't mean a lot to all the ducks and apples in the world."

"Did you become an Australian?" I asked.

She smiled. "Legally?"

"No, like Katherine Mansfield became an apple."

"My husband said I'd never be a dinkum Aussie. Not in a month of Sundays."

Her laughter overwhelmed me.

"And you?" she asked. "Are you a New Zealander?"

"It's too early to know," I said.

"Wasn't Katherine Mansfield a New Zealander?"

"New Zealanders like to think she was," I said.

"I think she was like us," Renata said. "She didn't belong anywhere. That's what I like about her. She wanted to belong to the world."

Coming upon Singapore from the sea was like opening my eyes on another world. I see it now, high white buildings through the humid haze, and narrow roads thronged with people, endless market stalls, the smell of street food, of open drains and durian! It was like the ending of Conrad's *Youth*. It was the beginning of my life.

Renata bought cotton blouses and sandals for her children. I followed her among the street stalls, astonished by everything around me—a man with yaws, his face a mess of pustules . . . a Chinese woman, bent double, inching her way painfully along the pavement . . . the roots of huge trees with walls of mildewed concrete in their grip . . . the rambutan rind underfoot, and gobbets of betel juice . . .

Every now and then we collapsed at a curbside table and ordered pork satay with rice cakes, Peking duck, and plates of kai choy by pointing at what other people were eating. Our plan was to drift in the general direction of Raffles Hotel, but every alley drew us down it, and though the children complained and wanted to be carried, Renata, like me, insisted we press on, that we see, taste, and explore everything.

It was late afternoon before we found Raffles Hotel. We bought

Singapore slings at the bar and Coca-Cola for the kids and went out beside the swimming pool, pretending to be hotel guests. The mere sight of the pool revived the children, who immediately stripped to their knickers and plunged in. Renata sat cross-legged under a fan palm, surveying the colonnades from behind her dark glasses. She was wearing a batik-print skirt and embroidered blouse. She seemed already to have become part of the place.

"I would like to stay here," I said. "Not here in the hotel. Maybe not even in Singapore. But somewhere like this."

"Why don't you?"

"Would you?"

"What—if I were you or if I were me?"

"If you were you."

"I have the children to think of. Before you have children, you're like an animal, always going out into the world, sussing things out. When you have children, you become like a tree, rooted to the ground. You grow upward and outward, but not for yourself. For them. To protect and nourish them."

Only ten minutes ago the children had been defeated by tiredness. Now they gamboled and splashed in the pool, shouting in Italian for their mother to join them.

"You see," Renata said, "what it is like?"

"Yes," I said, because I knew she was telling me that she wanted my friendship, nothing more.

I went into the hotel and bought another round of drinks. At the far end of the cocktail lounge was a group of passengers from the ship. Andy and Bill were accountants, Henry was a Rhodes scholar from Sydney. They recognized me and shouted at me to join them. They were waiting for dark when the nightclubs opened. One of the ship's officers had given them this address. You went to the club, bought a few beers, then you went on to this other place where there were sheilas. "Asian sheilas!" Andy exclaimed, clapping me on the shoulder. "You with us or against us?"

I went back to the pool with the drinks. Renata was toweling the children dry. I told her about running into Andy and Bill and Henry.

"Those losers," she said.

When Renata had dressed the children, they lay down beside her on the grass using our shopping bags as pillows. Renata caressed their heads, lulling them asleep. We sipped our drinks. Dusk came, then night. We sat together, cut off from the world, and shared our stories.

Renata was born on the day of *la festa della concezione immacolata.* Overnight, the first deep snow of the year had fallen. Above the village, the Brenta Massif was hidden in bruised cloud. In the bars, men were playing *briscola,* drinking wine, trading ribald stories, discussing the ski season that would soon be on them.

Three months ago, Renata's mother's brother had fallen to his death in the mountains while making an ascent of the Presanella. His name was Renato. He was fifteen years younger than his sister, and since their father's death in the same mountains she had raised him as though he were her child.

She knew of her brother's death the instant it happened. She was in the byre, milking. She felt drowsy and leaned forward against the flank of the cow. At that moment she was startled by the sound of someone behind her. As she turned, she heard her brother's voice. "It's me, Renato," the voice said. "I'm on the Presanella."

She got up from the milking stool and searched the byre. She strained to hear her brother's voice, willing him to speak again, but there was only the ringing silence of the night. But she had heard him distinctly, telling her he was on the Presanella. She stepped into the darkness. Across the valley a bull was bellowing. A dog barked. She looked toward the mountains, thinking his voice might have carried through the cold air. She could not believe that in her tiredness the noise of the animals moving in their stalls had tricked her into imagining her brother's voice. He had been so close. The voice had been so clear.

The following day, when news of the climbing accident reached the village, she walked alone up to the Nardis Glacier at the foot of the Presanella. She knew that the words she had heard were the last words her brother had spoken before he fell. He had been thinking of her.

Renata's mother was four months pregnant when her brother was killed. She became convinced that the child she was carrying would reincarnate him. The auguries were obvious. His name. His last words. Her dreams of a black bull.

Renata was born in the middle of May, under the sign of Taurus. The milk dried up in her mother's breasts. She complained that the baby was colicky and perverse, that it did not want to suckle. When the infant woke at night crying, it was her father who got out of bed and went to her. Her mother lay with her face to the wall, pretending to be asleep, longing to hear her brother's voice again, to know what he would do.

This is what Renata remembers of her childhood: The smell of cattle dung and straw in the byre, the cow nuzzling her with its wet black nose, its hot breath against her armpits, its abrasive, lolling tongue. The warm, creamy smell of fresh milk. The muslin parcels of spressa cheeses, the mostardo di frutta, and dried figs of Bari in their little straw boxes, which her mother force-fed her because they were "Renato's favorite food." Every Sunday, Renata goes to the cemetery with flowers. There is an oval photo of her uncle cemented to the tombstone. Renato is standing on a rocky spur with a rope coiled around his torso and an ice ax in his hand. Renata scrutinizes the blurred face, trying to fathom what it is he knows, what destiny he wishes on her. These are her thoughts long before her mother tells her that she was named after her uncle and that she should have been a boy.

One night, Renata's mother unlocks the small attic room that Renata has never entered. Renata is shown her uncle's climbing gear, his boots, his clothes. Her mother makes her stand in the middle of the room while she wraps an old tweed coat around her daughter's shoulders. When Renata discovers that her mother wants to make a coat for her from this heavy, musty cloth, she screams so loudly that neighbors call from the street, asking what is wrong. That is the day Renata tells her mother that she will never again enter a church. She describes the ex-votos in the chapel, the scenes of climbers falling from snow-capped peaks only to be saved by a saint sitting on a magic carpet of cloud high above the naively painted alpine landscape. She tells her mother, "If God intervened to save these other men, why did he let Renato die?" And then she calls her mother a fool for carrying a wreath up to the Nardis Glacier on the anniversary of Renato's death, for laying flowers on his grave and for continuing to believe he spoke to her just before he died.

Mealtimes become ordeals. Renata refuses to eat anything her mother puts in front of her. When her mother calls on her father to punish her, her father tells her to go to her room. Her sisters succumb to fits of giggles as Renata leaves the table, cursing them all. In her room, she plunges into a medieval romance, transported to another time and place. Later, her father comes and fetches her and takes her down to the village, where he buys her a bowl of minestrone. She is never happier than when sitting on a high stool in the Bar alla Torre while he sits among his friends drinking grappa. At home he never laughs. When he volunteers an opinion, he is cut off in mid-sentence by his wife, who then tells everyone what her husband really meant to say. Renata's sisters get into the habit of sighing and saying, "Oh Papa," whenever he opens his mouth to speak.

One day Renata is reading in her room when her father comes in to tell her he is going away. He is going to Germany to make a lot of money. Renata takes out a small brass box in which she keeps her trinkets. She gives her father all the coins in the box. He takes the child in his arms and tells her she does not understand.

He is gone for two years. While he is away, Renata is stricken with rheumatic fever. For a long time, the diagnosis is uncertain, and she is hospitalized in Trento. Her father comes back from Germany. He finds that his daughter has been put in a ward of old women, many of whom are dying. The child cries to be taken away from there, to be taken home.

"I think I always knew, from when I was a little girl, that I was supposed to be dead. That I didn't have a life of my own. My mother couldn't care less whether I lived or died. It was her brother she wanted to be alive, not me. And my father was already marked for the grave. He didn't have a life of his own, either. He had a favorite saying. Whenever I was miserable, he would hold me in his arms and say, "This too will pass, Renata." But then I began to realize that for him life itself had passed him by. He was just killing time, waiting for it to be over. He said, "I think that when I die, it will be in the mountains, in the snow. My body will never be found. And I will never be reborn. And no one will have to inherit the life I have failed to live.""

The Sinai war had ended five years ago, but when we came through the Suez there were still rusting hulks in the canal, gutted half-tracks in the desert, and MIG fighters in buff camouflage on airstrips among the date palms.

At Port Said, lighters came out to the *Fairstar* to take us ashore. A lot of passengers were heading off to Cairo. Renata and I were among those too broke to afford the excursion. Mario, however, had persuaded Renata to let him take the children to see the pyramids. That night they would return to the ship wearing little tarbooshes, beaming at their mother and showing her the cheap brassware "Uncle" Mario had bought them in Cairo.

Renata and I went ashore a few hours after the Cairo trippers had departed. She was agonizing over whether she had been right to let the children go off with Mario. I assured her Mario would take good care of them and give them a splendid time. Mario had owned a coffee shop in Melbourne and made a small fortune selling homemade pasta and Italian espresso machines. Now he was returning to his beloved Milano to go into business there. I could easily understand how Mario had been successful. He had this knack of getting you to confide in him what you most wanted to do with your life; then, every time he ran into you, he'd make you feel good by asking earnestly how things were working out and telling you anecdotes about all the people he knew who had dreamed of doing exactly what you dreamed of doing, and had got a lucky break and done it. And he'd always smile broadly and grip your arm, as if he really knew how you would fare in life. You'd warm toward him, even while telling yourself what a scoundrel he really was. "Slow and steady, maite," he'd say, in that ocker drawl he'd acquired. "Slow and steady wins the raice." My God! How could Renata have let her children go off with the little creep!

We were sitting in a café on the quayside, watching the lights on the water, when Hassan appeared. He was wearing a linen suit and carried a furled umbrella. Begging us to forgive the intrusion, he asked if he might steal a few minutes of our time. We invited him to sit down.

His demeanor changed immediately. He ordered lagers, insisting the waiter bring Foster's, then congratulated himself on guessing our nationalities. Neither Renata nor I corrected him. We had no plans to do anything in particular. We were within sight of the *Fairstar*. We were curious to know what he wanted.

"Might I demand a personal question?" Hassan ventured after we had followed him in raising our glasses to toast the health of all Australians.

"Certainly," Renata said.

Hassan directed his gaze to me. "Might I be so bold as to ask if you and the young lady are romantically engaged?"

Renata and I exchanged quick glances, trying not to smile. "We are friends," Renata said.

Hassan did not take his eyes off me. "Just friends?" he asked. "You are not married? You are not affianced?"

"Like the lady said," I said, "we are not affianced."

"Why do you ask?" Renata said.

"If you are not affianced or married, then there is something I will like to propose to you. You are a beautiful lady. You are an honorable man. It will be the easiest thing in the world for you to misunderstand me. But I am a businessman. This is purely business. I will tell you my situation. Then I will tell you what I propose. Please, do not be offended."

We heard him out. He was indeed a man of means. But not a socialist. He wanted to get his money out of Nasser's Egypt and invest it in Australia. "The land of opportunity," he called it. To accomplish this, he needed an Australian wife. The money could be made over to her and thus taken out of Egypt. For this "arrangement" the woman could expect generous recompense. There would be no strings attached. It was a straightforward business arrangement. When he had finished, he asked if he had offended the young lady.

I expected Renata to end the conversation by saying she was married. Instead, she asked him how she could be sure he would keep his side of the bargain? "How can I trust you?"

Hassan seemed surprised. If he had tried his scheme out on other Australian girls coming ashore in Port Said, this must have been the first time it had been taken seriously.

"We must spend more time talking. I have papers I will show you. We will share a meal. Everything will be at my expense. But we must move quickly, Mademoiselle. You see how ill-mannered a man can be when he has business on his mind? I do not even know your name."

"Renata" Renata said.

"Mademoiselle Renata," Hassan said.

I felt as if he had placed his hand on her thigh.

We drank more beer and ate shish kebabs and saffron rice. Then Hassan hailed a horse-drawn cab so I could be driven around the streets of Port Said while he and Renata discussed his deal.

I clip-clopped around the harbor for at least an hour, loathing Hassan and mad at Renata. What kind of game was she playing at?

"It wasn't a game," she told me later, when we were back on board the ship. "I was serious."

"Are you crazy?" I said. "You don't even know the guy. What if you got married to him and he sold you off to a harem or something as a white slave? Anyway, how could you marry him? You're married already!"

"No, I'm not. I threw my wedding ring into the sea when I left Melbourne."

"Throwing a wedding ring into the sea doesn't dissolve a marriage."

"You don't understand me," Renata said. "You're a man. You want to control women. You cannot let us choose our own path. We always have to go down the path you choose."

"Isn't Hassan a man?"

"You're jealous. You are ignorant and jealous!"

When the *Fairstar* docked at Genoa, I went to the railway station with Renata and the children. Mario was there, too, with his leather luggage and Egyptian souvenirs. It was true, I was ignorant and jealous, and the fact that Mario and Renata were traveling together on the same train to Milan was enough to convince me that Mario had used Renata's children to worm his way into her heart.

Renata and I had already exchanged addresses. Now there seemed nothing to say. I took her hands in mine and kissed her on the mouth. Then I kissed the children. When I made to shake Mario's hand, he clasped my head between his hands and kissed me. It was the final insult. I turned away. I wanted to be alone. I wanted to leave the last five weeks behind me. But I also needed desperately to hang on to them. Life on the *Fairstar* had been time out of time. Now everyone was dispersing. We were back in the real world again.

I kept Renata's address for four years. In all that time I never wrote to her and she never wrote me. But I'd often notice her address in my address book, hastily written in red ink, and I would try to conjure a memory of her face, only to find that I remembered more vividly the dark green carriages of the Paris *rapide* I boarded at Genoa, and the mountains in failing light as I crossed into France without the faintest idea how I would survive there.

I lived in France for a while, then England, then the Congo, and finally returned to New Zealand.

When I met Pauline, it was as if I had known her in a previous life. She resembled Renata, yes. Her mouth slightly pharaonic, her dark hair and eyebrows recalling film stars I had been drawn to as a boy, but there was more I could not identify, though I knew that everything I had seen and done in my life found expression in that split second of sudden light.

> You have been mine before,
> How long ago I may not know:
> But just when at that swallow's soar
> Your neck turn'd so,
> Some veil did fall,—I knew it all of yore.[2]

Pieces of Music

Some years ago, I happened to watch a rare film of Pablo Casals playing Bach's Suite No. 1 for cello. The film was shot in the Benedictine Abbey of Saint-Michel-de-Cuxa in southwest France in 1954. Casals was a refugee from Franco's Spain, and this was one of his first public performances after several years of silence.

Listening to the seventy-seven-year-old Casals, seemingly alone in this roofless French abbey, playing for no visible audience, I was reminded of a story that Norman Cousins tells in his *Anatomy of an Illness*. The story appealed to me because it hinged on the kind of synchronicity that is the magical glue that holds a narrative together and speaks to the mystery of how two people are sometimes fortuitously brought into each other's orbit at exactly the right time and in exactly the right place.

Almost thirteen years after the film was shot, and only a few months before Casals's ninetieth birthday, Cousins traveled to Puerto Rico, where the cellist and his wife Maria were now living. Although Don Pablo's favorite composer was Bach, and he owned several original Bach manuscripts, the cellist confided to his American visitor that his favorite composition was not by Bach, but by Brahms, and he offered to show Cousins the original manuscript of Brahms's B-flat Quartet—one of the world's most valuable music manuscripts still in private hands. After taking it down from the wall, where it had been framed behind glass, Casals told Cousins how the manuscript came into his possession.

Many years ago, Casals had formed a friendship with a man called Wilhelm Kuchs, head of the Friends of Music in Vienna. One night in Vienna before the war, Kuchs invited several friends for dinner, including Casals. Kuchs had one of the finest private collections of original music manuscripts in the world and owned an impressive collection of fine musical instruments, including violins by Stradivarius and Guarneri.

Following the Nazi annexation of Austria, and now in his nineties, Kuchs escaped to Switzerland, where Casals renewed their friendship. Though moved to see his old friend again, Casals was concerned about the fate of Kuchs's manuscripts and wanted to know if he had been able to keep them from falling into Nazi hands.

Not only had Kuchs saved his entire collection; he eagerly showed Casals several priceless pieces, beginning with chamber music by Schubert and Mozart. When Kuchs then placed on the table the original manuscript of the Brahms B-flat Quartet, Casals could hardly believe his eyes. He stood transfixed. "I suppose every musician feels that there is one piece that speaks to him alone," Casals told Cousins. "This was the way I had felt about the B-flat Quartet ever since I played it for the first time. And I always felt it was mine."

Seeing the emotional impact of the B-flat Quartet manuscript on Casals, Kuchs said, "It is your quartet in every way. It would make me very happy if you would let me give it to you."

Casals was so overcome by this unexpected gift that he could not find words to adequately thank his friend, though subsequently wrote a letter, telling him of the great pride and joy the gift had brought to his life. In response, Kuchs provided details about the B-flat Quartet that Casals had not known. "One fact in particular stood out," Casals told Cousins. "Brahms began to write the quartet just nine months before I was born. It took him nine months to complete it. We both came into the world on exactly the same day, the same month, the same year."

Does music often figure in synchronicity stories because it has such a power to evoke memories of distant times and places, bringing past and present together as if they were organically continuous and connected?

Consider, for instance, the following story about the great classical guitarist Andrés Segovia.

> Towards the end of a recital in Berlin, just as he was concluding with a *pianissimo*, there was a loud cracking noise. Segovia rushed off. Gregor Piatigorsky, who visited him backstage, found him muttering "my guitar, my guitar," as if it was the only word he knew.
>
> Sometime afterwards, Segovia told Piatigorsky that his friend who had made the guitar had died in Madrid at the precise moment the instrument had split in Berlin.[1]

While pieces of music precipitate vivid memories, musical instruments often embody the lives of those who played them. Intersubjectivity isn't, therefore, simply a word for the emotional connections that bind people together but for the ties that bind us to objects, heirlooms, and landscapes.

From the late 1960s, the professional violinist Geoffry Wharton worked in Europe and often played encores at his classical concerts, including "jazz pieces" by an obscure composer called Audrey Call. Although Wharton first discovered Call's music when he was a student at Sacramento State in 1969 and happened on some of her sheet music in the practice room, he had no idea how the music came to be there (he would later say, "There might have been some magic involved"). Nor did he know who Audrey Call was. Eventually, he wrote to Call's publisher in New York and was told that they had published three of her pieces in 1937 but had no biographical information about her. With the advent of the internet, Wharton finally got lucky. From an elderly record collector in London, he learned that Call had worked in several New York studio orchestras and appeared on various radio shows, including one called *Fibber McGee and Molly*. He also discovered that Call had been a virtuoso violinist in her youth, had studied at the Conservatoire de Paris, and had married the Italian-born bandleader Ulderico Marcelli.

Wharton then made a startling discovery. His mid-eighteenth-century Gagliano violin, which he had purchased in 1970, around the time he first encountered Audrey Call's music, *had once belonged to her*. Certificates of sale indicated that it was in her possession in 1945. "That was the moment," Wharton said, "that I realized there was a kind of cosmic connection between the pieces I've been playing all these years and the owner of my Gagliano violin."

The connections did not end there.

Wharton tracked down Call's son, Victor Marcelli, in San Francisco and paid him a visit. Victor described his mother's lifelong passion for sharing music with her students, her community, and the world. Victor then showed his visitor the violin his mother had played up to a few months before her death in 2001 and recalled her placing the instrument in its case for the last time and bidding her "old friend" goodbye. Victor then gave the violin to Geoffry Wharton as a gift, saying that in playing it his mother's music would continue to live on, a comment made even more poignant by the fact that nearly all her scores and published music had been lost when the shed in which the collection was stored was flooded.[2]

Strangers on a Train

On a recent trip back to my homeland I decided, for old times' sake, to take the overnight train from Wellington to Auckland. As I threaded my way through the crowded concourse of the Wellington Railway Station, I wondered at the hidden thoughts and feelings of the people flowing and eddying around me. All seemed bent on going somewhere and getting there without a moment's delay. All seemed oblivious to the urgency of other people's journeys, so that by the time I reached my platform and the crowd dispersed I had begun to ask myself where *I* was going, and why I had decided to take a train to Auckland rather than fly.

As the train lurched and shrieked through the switches in the marshaling yards, I became mesmerized by the tracks running in parallel before merging or disappearing beneath the train. And as the clack-clackety-clack began to mesmerize me, lines from Carl Sandburg's *Limited* came to mind.

> I am riding on a limited express, one of the crack trains of the nation.
> Hurtling across the prairie into the blue haze and dark go fifteen
> all-steel coaches holding a thousand people.
>
> (All the coaches shall be scrap and rust and all the men and women
> laughing in the diners and sleepers shall pass to ashes.)
>
> I ask a man in the smoker where he is going and he answers: "Omaha."

My last glimpse of Wellington before the train plunged into a tunnel was of the sea rasped by the southerly and the Orongorongos going indigo in the stormy light.

When it was no longer possible to see anything beyond my own reflection in the window, I brought my face closer to the pane, trying to peer through the reflected furnishings and fittings of the compartment. Unable to escape this looking-glass world, I snapped off the light. My own face was still discernible against the darkness outside, but I could now switch my focus from this shadow of myself to the steep black hillsides of the Kapiti coast and back again, figure to ground, ground to figure. It occurred to me that many non-Western peoples construe their reflections, shadows, and names as living extensions of themselves, so that a person's photograph can literally entrap or steal their souls—though we too speak of photographs capturing a person's likeness, and many people refuse to be photographed for fear that when the photo passes from their hands they lose control over their own destiny. Moreover, we all frame and enshrine photos or carry photos of our loved ones with us, as if photos keep our connections to them alive.

A small stream ran through the center of my hometown. In winter, after heavy rain, it often broke its banks and flooded the downtown streets. One year, our neighbors' small son was swept away and drowned. Two days passed before the body was recovered—stripped and snagged in a stand of willows half a mile downstream. His forehead was bruised, his skin was like pumice stone. Weed and silt dribbled from his nostrils and mouth.

The grief-stricken parents asked the mortician to make their son's face as lifelike as possible. The boy was embalmed, makeup applied to the face, and an expression-former crammed into his mouth to transform the rictus of death into the semblance of a smile. The dead boy was then dressed in his Sunday best, wedged in a chair and photographed. The photo was enlarged, colorized, and framed, and hung above the mantelpiece in their living room. I used to go to the house quite often. The dead boy was never mentioned. The colors in the photograph faded. The heavy frame collected dust, and I wondered if our neighbors' memory of their dead son had faded in sympathy.

After unlocking the mechanism that turned my seat into a bed, I undressed and slipped between the starched sheets. Pulling the thin blanket over me, I propped myself up on my elbow, looking out the window and trying to translate the silhouetted hills into a memory of landscapes I had passed through in daylight. The Manawatu plains ... drained swamplands, flax with seedpods like charred matchsticks ... morose herds huddled on waterlogged paddocks. Again, the clickety-clack of the wheels, the hollow wind-roar as the train crossed a culvert. So many journeys, to and fro in this narrow island, the same sinuous ridge in the darkness flowing, and memories rising from the land like mist.

My high school chemistry teacher was Rudie Nowak. At least that's the name I remember him by. He was Polish, pasty-faced, and always wearing the same brown linen suit. Sometimes he looked haunted, sometimes hunted; he presented no other face to the world. We never knew what brought him to our town, only what led to his departure. Perhaps, in the school that hired him after he was dismissed from ours, the story of his humiliation was forgotten, and he got the second chance we never gave him.

Remembering him, I felt no chagrin. I heard his nasal accent and saw him struggling to control our class with exasperated threats, reinforced with clumsily administered bursts of dry ice from a hand-held fire extinguisher, his only defense against our paper darts and gibes.

One summer, Nowak decides to go to Auckland by train. He needs a break from the chaos of the classroom, the corridors on rainy days stinking of egg sandwiches, apple cores, and orange peel. He wants to get as far away as possible from dung-spattered dairy herds and the ceaseless rain. He intends to check the job ads in the Auckland papers, perhaps quit teaching and find some less stressful work.

Having left it until too late to book a first-class seat (it is the school holidays), Nowak had to accept a last-minute cancellation in a second-class smoker.

After buying a pillow and newspaper, he prepares for a long night.

He sleeps fitfully and is jerked awake as the train pulls into a hissing moonlit hamlet where a Māori trudges up the line with a lantern, feet crunching on gravel, breath ghosting the air.

Lying back, Nowak places a hand over his eyes. He does not want to look at his wristwatch. He wants to forget about time. Then he is aware of someone standing over him, breathing heavily, and he takes his hand away from his eyes and sees a young woman wrestling to get her rucksack into the overhead rack.

Before Nowak can get up and offer assistance, she has crammed her rucksack into the rack beside Nowak's own battered attaché case. As she sits down beside him, Nowak apologizes for his slowness in realizing she needed help.

"I don't need any help," she says.

Her black hair is a tangle. She is wearing a black leather jacket and jeans. She unzips her jacket, takes it off, and spreads it across her chest. It comes up to her chin. She folds her arms under it. Nowak glances at the reservation ticket inserted in a brass fitting over the window frame. RESERVED: OHURA-HAMILTON.

"Might I ask if you are going far?" he says.

"As far as I fuckin' well can," she says.

"Your reservation card says Hamilton," he says.

"What's it to you? I'm going to Auckland. I just decided."

"Myself too," Nowak says. "I'm taking a holiday. It will be my first proper visit to Auckland. Is it your first time too?"

"Nope. Been there plenty of times."

"My name is Rudie Nowak," he says.

"Yeah,'" she says, as if he's pulling a fast one. She declares she's buggered and wants to sleep, and Nowak apologizes for disturbing her. He did not want to seem forward, but if one is traveling alone it is reassuring to know whom you are with.

"Sure," she says, and closes her eyes.

Nowak cannot sleep. He tries to steal a glance at her in the window, but he sees only his own woeful face, his balding head, his manifest loneliness. He glances swiftly at her. She is already asleep. *That is good*, he thinks. *She isn't afraid of me, she feels comfortable sitting with me, sharing with me this journey through the night.*

At Taumarunui, a Combined Services rugby team and a throng of fans board the train. They are wearing identical blazers and scarves. They push down the narrow aisle with their duffel bags and guitars, looking for their seat numbers. Nowak wipes the condensation from the window with the palm of his hand. In the darkness, he sees women in greatcoats, their arms folded tightly across their breasts. They stamp to keep warm. There are flurries of snow. Nowak has the impression that everyone is fed up with the prolonged goodbyes, standing around in the cold in the dead of night.

Some of the footballers are blocking the aisle where Nowak and Sally are sitting. Others are trying to push past. They stare at Sally. Some of them grin and look back at their mates. One says, "How yer goin'?"

Nowak hears the clink of bottles.

"Footballers," he says to Sally.

"Tell me about it," she says.

Two men with glazed eyes and florid faces take the seat opposite. One hauls a bottle of beer out of his duffel bag. His mate yanks the cap off with his teeth.

"Wanna drink?" he asks, holding the bottle out to Sally.

"Sure, why not."

Nowak stiffens. *Why does she talk to him; why does she accept this drink from him?*

"Excuse me," he says to Sally. "But perhaps you would prefer to sit by the window and let me take the aisle seat."

Sally prefers no such thing.

"Cigarette?" says the man opposite.

When Sally thanks him, Nowak has difficulty believing this is happening.

"Where you from?" the footballer asks.

Sally lights her cigarette and blows smoke into the seatback in front of her.

"Palmerston North," she says, "origin'ly."

"Yeah?" the footballer says. "I worked down at Shannon for a bit. Out at the hydro."

It seems the footballer, like Nowak, is prepared for this conversation. He takes a swig of beer. His blazer rides up, disclosing his podgy midriff.

"So what you do for a living?" he asks.

"I don't," Sally says.

"Eh?"

"I don't do anything for a living. I'm waiting for my life to start happening."

"Oh yeah?"

Nowak thinks, *Now I understand. It's her ruse for getting rid of him, being friendly and threatening at the same time so he'll leave her alone of his own accord.* He observes the footballer in the window, notices the nonchalant way she smokes the cigarette he gave her. Nowak is overcome with happiness. *I was right*, he says to himself, *I was right.*

Then the footballer is stretching across in front of Sally and grabbing at Nowak's arm.

"Beer, mate?"

"No, no thank you very much."

"Just trying to be friendly."

The footballer is forced back into his seat by the slam and jolt of the train moving off.

Nowak cannot look Sally in the eyes. He has to imagine the curious conflation of candor and cynicism in her gaze. He says to her, "I too am waiting for my life to start happening."

"That a fact," she says, and stubs out her cigarette.

"When I came to New Zealand," Nowak continues, "I left everything behind me. I wanted to make a clean breast of everything. I wanted to begin anew, with a clean slate. It is like dying, to be so reborn."

"Living in Palmerston North was like death warmed up," Sally says. "That's for sure."

Nowak chuckles. "You laugh about your predicament. That's good. That's healthy."

The footballers across the aisle climb to their feet. "Party time!" one says, and asks Sally if she wants to join them.

Sally ignores him.

"See you later alligator," the footballer says.

The footballer tucks his shirt in. His mate pulls some bottles of Lion Red out of his duffel bag in the overhead rack. Then they move off, cigarettes in their mouths, squinting through the smoke.

Now we are alone, Nowak thinks, *now we will not be disturbed.* He encourages her to talk about Palmerston North and what she meant by "death warmed up."

She talks some but is clearly distracted by the footballers boozing and singing *Dance, dance, dance to my ten guitars* at the other end of the carriage.

"You want to join them?" Nowak asks.

"Nah," she says. "Went to three parties last week. I don't want to get pissed again. Not with those blokes anyway."

"Your parents, they live in Palmerston North?" Nowak inquires.

"Yes and no," Sally says.

Nowak waits for her to go on.

"It's a long story," she says. "You wouldn't wanna hear about it."

"I would be honored to hear about it," Nowak says.

It is only now that Nowak observes the scar on her forehead. Sally reads his mind. "I was eighteen," she says. "My mother was a drunk. My father was in and out of hospital for some kind of cardiac condition. Every time he went in, my mother told me he could conk out at any time. She'd ask me what I would do if he did. She'd say, "If he dies, that's the end of me. You'll have to fend for yourself. I don't want to frighten you, I just want you to be prepared." So I prepared. I learned to cook my own meals. I learned to smoke. I learned how to get into the pub. One night, in the rain, in a car going too fast, driven by a boy who'd had too much to drink, we hit a bridge. I went through the windscreen. They stitched me up. But they couldn't mask the evidence of my mistake. I would look at myself in the mirror, hating what I saw. It took me months before I would venture out. I did not want to be seen. If someone looked at me hard I would want to shrink away and disappear down a drain. I drank to obliterate my shame. I became a party girl, a one-night stand, an easy lay. And then I met Johnny. The first man who showed me any kindness. My disfigurement did not matter to him. I was an angel. Poor loveable idiot. I was flattered. He looked after me. He took me seriously. He loved me, and I loved him. Isn't that what we do when we are loved? Love back. Give back what we are given? Set things straight?"

"What happened to Johnny, if I may ask?"

"You can ask. But I can't tell you. I can only tell you he's not with me."

"And your parents?"

Sally shrugs. *They were shriveled and black inside like bad walnuts. They had nothing to nourish me with or give. I don't know what went wrong for them, what made them want to keep the blinds drawn in the living room, I don't really care. They had nothing going for them, but why make me nothing too? Why, if they were withered up and black and crumbled inside like a fireplace that hasn't been cleaned or a dead walnut, did they pretend to be parents to me, yet pay me no mind and keep me from knowing who I am? I wanted the doll, they said I would break it if they let me have it; I wanted a puppy, they wouldn't let me have a dog, dogs stank the house out when they got wet in winter and came inside they said and were a problem when you went away, but since when did we ever go anywhere? The only things I had were the things I made up and hid from them, the things I thought of when I heard the train whistle in the hills at night or when I crawled through the bush by the river at Ashhurst and came to that sandy beach where no one ever came and the boulders were hot in the sun and there were dragonflies hovering over the water and trout rose to the surface, or at the riverhole with the others when the Wilsons' dog came splashing out into the shallows and stood there yelping and barking silly bugger while we all laughed because we'd all swum out into the deep part and Charlie didn't want to swim out too . . .*

Nowak is also alone with his thoughts. *Now I know it's not a coincidence or chance. Now I know we were destined to meet on this train tonight, we were meant to find each other.*

Then Sally tells him about the Dresden doll that had belonged to her adoptive mother and she wasn't allowed to play with, only look at, and how one day she took the doll and drowned it in the river. She tells Nowak she never wants to bring a child into this world. A child has no choice. "Why would we bring children into this world? It is full of cruelty and injustice. People make use of each other," she says. "It's dog eat dog. If you want to know my philosophy of life, it's get the other bugger before he gets you."

"You wish you had never been born," Nowak says. "Is that what you are saying?"

"That's exactly what I'm saying," she says.

Nowak bites his lip. His body is rigid. He stares straight ahead at the folded newspaper in the sagging string seat pocket.

"Heh," Sally says brightly. "Heh, you're from Germany, aren't you?"

Nowak prepares to hear more about dog eat dog.

"Am I right?" she says.

"Actually, I'm from Poland. Cracow to be precise."

Nowak thinks of her as a child, as a pupil in one of his classes. *It's like talking to a child,* he thinks.

Then she says, "So what kind of childhood did you have? Was it happy?"

"My father owned some land," Nowak says. *That life now lost to me, behind me, blurred.*

"So you grew up on a farm?"

Nowak smiles, "Well, not really."

"What then? What do you remember about it?"

He remembers something that happened when he was five and his older brother seven.

A peasant owed Nowak's father some money. Nowak's father took the peasant's donkey and said he would give it back when the peasant paid his debt. This was a blow to the peasant, who was too poor to own a milk cow and depended on his donkey for milk.

Nowak's father put the peasant's donkey into the field where he kept his own donkeys. He told his sons to give it some hay.

That evening, after feeding the peasant's donkey, Nowak and his brother decided to milk it. They figured that taking the donkey's milk would help compensate their father for the money he had not been paid. But they didn't realize there were both male and female donkeys in the field, and that they had caught the wrong one.

The donkey's penis extended and gave its "milk." They tasted it. It was salty, and not at all like cow's milk. Still, it would teach the peasant a lesson if he lost not only his donkey but his daily milk supply, and they redoubled their efforts to milk the donkey dry.

When they were done, they were troubled that the penis did not return to its original size and shape. "You've spoiled it," Nowak's brother said. "Now the peasant will know someone has tampered with his donkey. Now he will be demanding compensation from father!" They waited in the dusk, but the injured penis remained unchanged.

That night they could not sleep for worrying about what they had done and what their father would say in the morning.

"You can just imagine our relief," Nowak says, "when we went out to feed the donkey and found it had gone back to normal! We really laughed then, thinking how we'd deprived that poor peasant of his donkey milk!"

"Did that really happen?" Sally asks.

Nowak is chuckling again. "Yes, just as I told it to you!"

"Yuck!"

The silence descends like a snare. Nowak shrinks away. He begins to frame an apology in his mind but knows that whatever he says will only makes matters worse. And besides, the girl has turned away and drawn her leather jacket up over her shoulder, folding her arms, feigning sleep.

He hardly moves all night. She sleeps beside him. When the train pulls in at Frankton Junction, she remains asleep. Carefully, he climbs over her and joins the crowd sleepwalking toward the refreshment room.

He buys two cups of tea and two pieces of fruitcake. He decides she will want fruitcake rather than a meat pie at that hour of the morning. Balancing the crockery, he makes his way back along the platform to Car J.

At first, he thinks he must have got the wrong carriage. Then he spots his bag in the overhead rack and sees that her rucksack has gone. He sets the cups down on the floor, the tea slopping into the saucers. He pushes his way back down the aisle. He clutches the metal railing at the carriage door and leans out. He looks up and down the platform, but she has vanished.

A few weeks later, the following story appears in the *Taranaki Herald*.

LOVE ON THE LIMITED

A chance meeting last August has turned into a solitary vigil for Rudolph Nowak.

The high school chemistry teacher is seeking a woman he has met only once and whose first name may be Sally.

They shared the same seat on the Limited one winter night. Both were traveling to Auckland, he for a holiday, she in search of work.

"There was such a natural affinity between us," said Mr. Nowak. "We were kindred spirits. It was something we both recognized."

Yet the couple failed to exchange addresses, and Nowak has now exhausted every possibility of locating his lost love.

He has even placed advertisements in newspapers countrywide. One advertisement in *Truth* cost him $200. "Calling Sally. I love you. Where are you?" it read and gave his name and telephone number. But so far the advertisement has attracted only ridicule. "Now I am obliged to leave the phone off the hook at night," Nowak said, "otherwise I get no sleep."

Nowak came to New Zealand from Poland two years ago. He hoped to make a new life here. Now he feels fate has passed him by. "If I don't find her, I don't know what I will do," he said. "My life has no meaning without her. This wasn't just a case of strangers on a train."

In our class, the newspaper clipping is passed fervently from hand to hand. We relish its derisive undertone. Nowak has only to cross the school quadrangle or enter a classroom to be assailed by catcalls. During one class, a train whistles in the distance, and Nowak uses up an entire fire extinguisher in his desperation to shut us up. There is so much dry ice on the benches that it looks as if a snowstorm has hit the room. We make wisecracks about the chemistry of love, and the whole class collapses into laughter when Nowak calls the roll and has to ask if Sally Faulkner is present.

I woke to find that we were still in the King Country. It was first light, and the train was following the course of a river. I was thinking about New Zealand as John Mulgan described it in his *Report on Experience*, the country "so old in itself that none of us have dared touch it; we have only just begun to live there. . . . We could leave it ourselves now. In a few years the red-roofed wooden bungalows would rot with borer and crumble into the earth."

I also remembered how Mulgan wrote of the emptiness of the land and the conflict that rose in New Zealanders because of it, because "there have never been enough of them nor have they had sufficient confidence in themselves to take over the country, so that they live there like strangers or as men might in a dream which will one day wake and destroy them. . . . This is one reason why New Zealanders, a young people but already with a place in history, are often wanderers and restless and unhappy men. They come from the most beautiful country in the world, but it is a small country and very remote. After a while this isolation oppresses them and they go abroad. *They roam the world looking not for adventure but for satisfaction.*"

As I recalled Mulgan's lines, I became aware of the railway lines in the early morning light, running in parallel, merging, separating, merging again, and I thought of lost love, lost time, lost talents, lost friends, lost hopes, and wondered for the first time in many years what on earth became of Nowak and Sally after their coincidental meeting on the same overnight train.

More mysterious than the synchrony of events in time and space is the mystery of why some people set such great store by coincidences, divining in them the hidden hand of fate, while others write them off as meaningless and banal. It is impossible for me to know why Rudolph Nowak attributed such significance to his chance encounter with Sally, laying himself open to romantic disappointment and public ridicule. But the pathos of his story has stayed with me for many years, as if I too, despite my avowed realism, find in his innocent fantasy an enviable faith.

The Lost Child

Many people experience such a deep connectedness with the natural world that they speak of it as a form of love. Certainly, I have always felt this way about the sea. It is synonymous in my imagination with the unconscious, and with the most joyous days of my childhood.

Although I grew up in a land-locked town, I would often spend my school holidays with my favorite aunt and uncle, whose house stood on an immense sand dune overlooking the ocean. I would fall asleep listening to the waves hiss and sigh in the darkness, and every day after breakfast I would clamber over the stile at the end of my uncle's garden and follow a sandy path along the railway line that connected New Plymouth with its port. Sometimes I would place pennies or pebbles on the tracks and wait for the port train to flatten them. Mostly though, I would press on, stepping from sleeper to sleeper over the rust-colored ballast until I came to where the path reentered the dunes, now thick with broom, marram, pampas, and lupin. The broom pods explode in the noonday heat. I breathe in the honey-heavy odor of lupin. Bumblebees hover. Flies buzz. Moving quickly now, because the iron sand has made me a firewalker, I follow the narrow track into the heart of the dunes. There I enter a silence so complete and comforting that I still conjure it as a sanctuary. I hesitate.

One step forward and I will hear the sea. The uproar of the world. One step back and the sea will be silenced. I push on, and the sea is instantly in my ears, its sound indistinguishable from the coursing of the blood inside my head. I inhale a mingling of brine and kelp that is like the sweat one licks from the body of one's beloved. And the ocean is rolling ashore, lacerated on the black volcanic reef, while a single sweep of iron sand leads my eye from the sugarloaves in the south to the white cliffs in the north. My heart swells with the promise of life.

Several images coincide and chime as I recall those days along the New Plymouth foreshore, including Ernest Shepherd's illustration for A. A. Milne's "Sand between the Toes" in *When We Were Very Young*, and e. e. cummings's line that "whatever we lose like a you or a me / it's always ourselves we find at the sea."

Perhaps it was to recapture my childhood that I drove to Karekare Beach to walk on iron sand and inhale the ozone from the open sea. Perhaps it was simply to get some respite from Auckland city after giving my seminar on the mask.

After parking my rental car near a cliff of black conglomerate, I passed a waterfall wedded to the rock and a stream flowing through a glade of pōhutukawa. A track led through dunes to the ocean beach.

Along the track a woman was calling to her child. Her voice was shrill and panicked. On seeing me, she explained that her little girl was lost, and she begged me to help find her. Rather than try to comfort the frantic mother, I stumbled through the marram and lupin toward higher ground. In the distance I could see the father running hither and thither, also calling the name of his daughter at the top of his lungs. I hoped he had checked the stream in case his daughter had gone there. It was the only place of danger I could see. Then, as suddenly as she had disappeared, the child reappeared, walking oblivious out of the sandhills in a red sunhat. I called to the father, who was still running around like a headless chicken. "She's here! She's been found!" The mother enfolded her daughter in her arms, speaking her name over and over, sotto voce, as if to calm herself, while the child, innocent of the distress she had caused, asked for an ice cream.

I went on to the beach and walked barefoot over the wet iron sand. The headland was ghosted with spume. Picnickers and surfers strolled to or from the ocean. The sun was hot.

At that moment, I found myself remembering the tragic story of David Wright.

Internationally known for his monographs on Yeats's myth of self and Joyce's sense of irony, Wright had also written a book on the unsolved mystery of the *Joyita*, a sixty-nine-foot wooden fishing boat that vanished on a voyage between Apia, Western Samoa, and Fakaofo in the Tokelau Islands in October 1955 when he was three.

Joyita: Solving the Mystery was published in 2002, six years before David Wright's death at the age of fifty-six. From the very first page of this book, one is struck by the uncanny parallelism between the doomed ship and the author's own troubled life. "It is debatable," Wright says, "whether some ships are ill-fated, but for much of its life the *Joyita* was certainly associated with more than its share of trouble and sadness; joy was a quality seldom attached to it."[1]

David had suffered depression for many years, and after the breakup of his marriage, he tried to kill himself by jumping from a two-story building. He survived, with two broken legs, and as he healed physically, he also seemed to recover his mental stamina. Then his mother, Fay, to whom he was deeply attached, became ill. David felt guilty that he could not spend as much time with her as he wished, and after her death he fell again into deep depression. Unable to sleep, he sought medical help, but the prescribed antidepressant only exacerbated the problem. Though David and his father had never been particularly close, Graham Wright now came to live with his son, to keep him company and, hopefully, lift his spirits. But the two men had little to say to each other and watched videos together rather than talk. One morning, Graham woke to find his son missing. The only trace of him was a pile of brine-soaked clothing on the laundry floor. It was later deduced that David had attempted to drown himself off Milford Beach, but failed. He came home, stripped off the sodden clothes, and dressed in heavier garments with deep pockets that he could fill with stones. Now weighed down, he was able, finally, to extinguish his pain and end the dreadful night.

David Wright's connections with the *Joyita* only compounded the mystery of his tragic death.

In his preface to *Joyita*, he explains that his interest in the fate of the *Joyita*'s passengers and crew began with his parents' speculations about the fate of Fay's first cousin, Roger Pearless, who was one of the disappeared. Pearless was a district officer in the Tokelau Islands in 1955, though based in Apia. "It was largely at his urging that the voyage took place."[2]

In the late 1990s, David Wright began intensive archival research in the hope of tracing relatives and descendants of some of the disappeared. Because his academic field was Irish literature, he became fascinated by Alfred Denis Parsons, an Irish physician who had been traveling to Tokelau to perform an emergency amputation on a patient there.

At about the time he began his research, David happened to read a newspaper story about the Irish novelist Julie Parsons who was visiting New Zealand for the first time in thirty-six years. Julie was Alfred Parsons's daughter. David wrote to Julie, now back in Dublin, explaining his interest in the *Joyita* and initiating an exchange of letters in which they discussed the mystery and shared their stories. A month later, he met Julie's brother, Simon, also on a visit to New Zealand, and in January 2000 he wrote to Julie's sister, Gay Johnson, another Dubliner, "to see if she had any further thoughts on the case."[3] Gay offered some detailed personal recollections of the time of the disaster, and of her childhood in Samoa. She vividly recalled farewelling her father when he left on the voyage, and the moment when her family was first notified that the boat was overdue.

After "a prolific email correspondence," in which David and Julie "felt moved to talk about many other matters," they discovered intriguing coincidences that David was tempted to interpret as auguries: the fact, for instance, that Gay lived almost within sight of Joyce's tower, which he knew well but had never visited, and that their families had lived in the same suburb of Torbay in the 1950s. "It was clear that we were becoming fond of one another. We made phone calls and exchanged photographs, then arranged to meet in San Francisco in April 2000."[4]

Another meeting followed in Ireland that June, and they visited Joyce's tower together. With their marriage later that year, Gay sensed that her life had come full circle, and David expressed the view that there was "something remarkable about all these circuitously patterned events" and the way they disclosed "a sense of the quirky possibilities of fate." He then concludes: "It does seem that a happy ending has been fashioned at last from one strand of an old tragedy. And after loving Ireland and Irish literature for the past two decades, it seems wonderfully strange that I should finally marry an Irishwoman solely because I happened to begin investigating a boat whose people vanished forever in a remote corner of the Pacific Ocean more than 45 years ago."

Despite being attentive and sensitive to the quirkiness of fate, David Wright's newfound happiness could not eclipse the dark mystery that still haunted his life, hovering on the margins, eating away at his soul. Indeed, the checkered history of the *Joyita* reads like an allegory of David's own life.

"The boat began its life in Los Angeles in 1931 as a luxury yacht, and a number of movie stars sailed on it. One of them, Thelma Todd, died in suspicious circumstances; it has even been alleged that she was murdered by the *Joyita*'s first owner, Roland West, who was her lover at the time. Later the *Joyita* served with the United States Navy in Hawaii as a patrol boat during the Second World War, traveled to many remote Pacific Islands, spent several years in Samoa as a fishing vessel and in Fiji as a copra ship, ran aground three times altogether, and was briefly owned by Robin Maugham, whose quest to end its ill luck by exorcism went all the way to the Archbishop of Canterbury."

What tips a life toward joy or despair is not necessarily something we do or say; it is commonly something over which we have no control and cannot have foreseen. No one felt this more acutely than David Wright. For at the very moment he was struggling with depression after his mother's death, his wife, Gay, and their small son, Gabriel, were obliged to return to Ireland where Gay's stepfather was dying. Gay's absence may have been the last straw and, fatefully, word of David's suicide reached Gay on the day of her stepfather's funeral.

Thanks largely to David Wright's painstaking research, there proved to be no great mystery to the disappearance of the crew and passengers of the *Joyita*, merely a tragic set of circumstances born of negligence, bad luck, and panic. The poorly maintained marine engines broke down, a serious leak caused the boat to list, an SOS transmission failed because of a disconnected aerial, and the crew and passengers abandoned ship in darkness, omitting to tether their Carley floats to the drifting vessel. By dawn they would have lost sight of the ship, which did not sink, and they perished through dehydration, exposure, exhaustion, and, in all probability, shark attacks. "It is distressing to imagine what thoughts went through their minds during their final hours," writes David Wright. But "they must have had enough time to come to the sad realization that nobody would ever know just what had happened to them."[5]

Is coincidence a synonym for fate? Does the past determine who we are and what we can become, or does everything depend on whether or not we grant the past this kind of power over us? Was David Wright's death by drowning the apotheosis of a series of events that included his mother's cousin's death in the Pacific? And did David Wright read his own fate into *The Wasteland* ("Phlebas the Phoenecian a fortnight dead"), or Virginia Woolf's suicide in 1941, permitting us to find in Virginia's last note to her husband something of what David experienced in his last hours?

> Dearest, I feel certain I am going mad again. I feel we can't go through another of those terrible times. And I shan't recover this time. I begin to hear voices, and I can't concentrate. So I am doing what seems the best thing to do. You have given me the greatest possible happiness. You have been in every way all that anyone could be. I don't think two people could have been happier till this terrible disease came. I can't fight any longer. I know that I am spoiling your life, that without me you could work. And you will I know. You see I can't even write this properly. I can't read. What I want to say is I owe all the happiness of my life to you. You have been entirely patient with me and incredibly good. I want to say that—everybody knows it. If anybody could have saved me it would have been you. Everything has gone from me but the certainty of your goodness. I can't go on spoiling your life any longer.

Each human life shades into others. There is no finite point at which one ends and another begins, no way of working out who is who in the distorting mirrors of genealogical time. But there is a world of difference between saying that our lives are products of the past and saying that each life echoes what has gone before without ever being completely explained by it. That David Wright turned to researching the *Joyita* story during the darkest days of his own life suggests that no human being is ever in a position to identify the source of his or her fate; all we can do is tell our story obliquely through the lives of others, and the projects that inexplicably compel our interest.

In the Nature of Things

In his explorations of psychoanalysis and the occult, George Devereux observes that correspondences between the thoughts of people who are in an intimate relationship with each other are bound to occasionally coincide. For us to respond to this sympathetic overlapping with wonderment is understandable, but are we justified in concluding that we are dealing with a unique, sui generis phenomenon that science cannot explain? That many people will assign special meanings to certain numbers, like 13 (bad luck) and 3 (third time lucky), may tell us more about those individuals than the phenomenon itself. For this reason, Devereux adopts a skeptical attitude toward such psi-phenomena as telepathy and telekinesis, preferring to ask why a person should become obsessed by these occurrences or develop outlandish theories and compulsive practices on the strength of them.[1]

Earlier, I touched on the relationship between *coincidence* as an unlikely conjunction of events in space and time and *affinity* as an affective bond between close kin or kindred spirits. I also mentioned a series of fateful dreams in which several old friends appeared to me, together with landscapes and periods of my life for which I felt an overwhelming nostalgia. These experiences reminded me of Devereux's observation that a "psychological rule says that when an inner situation is not made conscious, it happens outside, as fate."

But why should I remember Kamla Kant Pandey with such portentous clarity? And why now?

Kamla was head of the Genetics Unit at the Department of Scientific and Industrial Research during the years that I was teaching anthropology at Massey University. Although we lived in the same town, our workplaces were a quarter of a mile apart, and our social circles did not overlap, so I am mystified about how we came to meet, though not by the close friendship that developed between us.

Born in Varanasi in 1926, Kamla showed signs of genius in elementary school, writing a paper on "seed dispersal" for his agricultural science class that led his teacher to declare that this shy boy had independently discovered Darwin's theory of evolution.[2] Destined for greatness, at least in the eyes of his teacher, Kamla became the first Indian agriculture graduate to win the London Exhibition Scholarship. He subsequently joined the John Innes Institute in London to pursue research on plant genetics, and after completing his PhD in 1954, he and his wife, Kanti, settled in New Zealand. In 1966 he was elected Fellow of the Linnaean Society of London, and four years later was awarded the degree of DSc by the University of London.

During the years of our friendship, we would meet regularly and go for long cross-country hikes, talking about yoga, which I was practicing assiduously, and his research. Often, at the end of a windswept, rainy afternoon in the hills, my wife, Pauline, would join me as dinner guests of Kanti and Kamla and their children. I got used to Kanti serving us Indian vegetarian meals but never joining us at table, and Kamla excusing himself before dessert was served in order to drive to his lab and check on his experiments. He was working day and night on a revolutionary genetic modification technique known as "mutation breeding" in which seeds are irradiated in order to separate out undesirable genes and keep the desirable ones, which could then be bred with other cultivars. A breakthrough in 1975 was hailed as the most important discovery by a New Zealander since Lord Rutherford split the atom. But even as Kamla was making significant progress, researchers at the University of California were pioneering a very different process of genetic engineering in which pieces of recombinant DNA were transferred from one organism to another. Within ten years (in 1982), human insulin was synthesized from genetically engineered *E. coli* bacteria, the first genetically engineered human medication approved by the FDA, thereupon ushering in an era in which scientists confidently predicted that GM technology promised radical advances in controlling pests, improving crop yields, and treating diseases in humans.

Kamla did not live to see his own research initiatives supplanted by these new developments. He died at age fifty-nine, the same age that his son Rakesh died in 2018. Rakesh liked to say that "a person's life is like a jigsaw puzzle...it's about finding the right pieces and fitting them together." Kamla would undoubtedly have shared this view, though as a dedicated scientist rather than a devoted father. Indeed, I doubt that Kamla would have been given the obituary that Rakesh received after his death, celebrated as a loving father and caring mentor whose expertise in learning helped countless individuals qualify for university study.[3] But Kamla had his own favorite phrase. He repeated it so often in the course of our conversations that I presumed it summarized his philosophy of life. *It is in the nature of things*, he would say, as if everything from the evolution of life on earth to our own destinies were out of our hands. Our planet was a result of a series of accidents over several billion years. There was neither purpose nor design at work in it. Our species emerged by chance. Nothing was *meant* to be as it is. No natural or supernatural privilege gives us the right to impose our will on the world, to dominate other life forms, to exploit the earth as if everything is there solely for our benefit. Our abrogation of God's alleged omnipotence may be the undoing of us, and that we even conjure the idea of a God in our own image as an omniscient planner, moral arbiter, and supreme designer is a sure sign of how we invert reality to sustain the illusion of ourselves as masters of the universe.

I now think I might have misinterpreted Kamla's invocation of "the nature of things" for in riffling through my journals from the 1970s I am reminded of how ardently he embraced the Hinduism of his earliest years.

One day he confided a dream he'd had not long after his mother's death. The dream had left a lasting impression on him, and that I wrote it into my journal suggests that it also moved me.

He had dreamed he was carrying a corpse to a pyre by the river. The body was shrouded in colored cloth, and he knew then it was his mother.

When he woke, words were being forced from his throat, words so wild and terrible that he was sure he would be overheard on the street and people come running. *Ram naam satya hai, hare ram naam satya hai* he cried. The name of the Lord is the only reality!

I think Kamla's life's work, bombarding genes with radiation while dreaming of a Nobel Prize, brought home to me a choice I would have to make, between aspiring to an abstract goal and caring for those I loved. To what or to whom do we dedicate ourselves? Our families and friends, or some "higher" good, articulated as a religious faith, a moral ideal, or a work of art?

Il Ritorno in Patria

In bringing together a random set of stories in which coincidence plays a vital role, both structurally and substantively, I have been brought to address the question of what coincidences mean. Yet the very notion of meaning has proven to be problematic. Insofar as intellectuals associate "meaning" with logos, they often privilege phenomena that can be conceptually grasped, put into words, or confidently grasped. Experiences that slip through the fingers of the rational mind are, consequently, often written off as ineffable or grudgingly accepted as having a secondary role to play in human affairs. Hence the elevation of science over religion, abstract ideas over practical experience, and reason over superstition. The phenomenon of synchronicity challenges these distinctions, and demands a sociogenic rather than logocentric approach to the question of what it means to speak truth to life.

It is practically impossible to apprehend our experience directly. This is as true of our dreams, emotions, and intimate relationships, as it is of historical events. Experience only becomes intelligible and shareable when it is converted, through secondary elaboration, into conceptual or narrative form. Whether our theories and stories correspond to reality or are faithful to the facts of experience is, for me, a less compelling issue than the question of how our creative responses to events make our lives more livable. Meaning is therefore less a matter of understanding life or even explaining it. It is first and foremost a matter of creating a viable and congenial life for ourselves and for those we love.

I began this book by exploring Jung's thesis that synchronicities afford us insights into mythical leitmotifs and archetypes embedded deep within our collective unconscious. Rather than focus on coincidences as irruption of primordial images into everyday awareness, I preferred to explore the constellation of biographical and social elements that influence a person's perception of a coincidence. I first considered the hypothesis that human beings seek pattern and order in their lives as well as in the world around them, and I suggested that this quest for order is most imperative at times of personal crisis or social chaos. This led me to consider coincidences as constructed or imagined as much as naturally occurring. As such they function as discursive devices for creating the appearance of coherence in a disconnected world, or simply as means of bridging the gap between episodes in a story, as when a storyteller falls back on such stock phrases as "It so happened that," or "As chance would have it." I then argued that coincidences offered something more than confirmations of an order underlying empirical reality. They hold out the hope that shattered lives might be restored to health, hopes realized, and dreams come true. As a form of symbolic thinking, synchronicity deploys objective coincidences to vicariously realize emotional desires—the redressing of an old injustice, the healing of a psychological wound, the reconciliation of estranged friends, and even the reunion of the living and the dead. Instead of seeing coincidence stories as evidence of a need for either conceptual order or narrative coherence, I glimpsed in them fantasies of redemption, and poetic and natural justice.

One of the first coincidence stories I cited exemplified this theme.[1] Coincidentally, it closely resembled a story my mother-in-law, Petra, shared with me in 1994.

Petra employed a handyman to help with the yard work at her Raglan home. She and Tom became good friends and often shared details of their lives that they did not divulge to their respective families. Tom's first marriage ended when he left his wife for another woman who he subsequently married. Twelve years later, he left his second wife, Rose, for yet another woman. Rose began drinking heavily. Arrested for drunk driving, her license was revoked. Undeterred, she had tinted windows fitted in her car to avoid being recognized by the local police and continued driving under the influence. One day, having failed to close the car door properly before driving off, she actually fell out of the vehicle, which careened into a nearby house. The court ordered that she be hospitalized for detoxification. After reading about these events in the local newspaper, Tom visited Rose in the hospital. To his surprise and dismay, the woman in the bed next to Rose was his first wife—the woman he had left, together with their four children, to be with Rose. Seeing his first wife again, Tom was filled with remorse. He left his current paramour and moved to the Bay of Islands with his first wife.

I assumed that Petra would conclude this sad story by judging Tom harshly and pitying both Rose and the woman he had abandoned Rose to be with. But Petra's emphasis was on redressing an original sin, and this put me in mind of Keti Ferenke's stories about remembering and honoring the first things in life, the past made present again, the broken circle made whole.

In the image of coincidence, constancies of time, space, and personhood are annulled. What was once sundered is restored. The prelapsarian is recovered.

These reflections brought me full circle to the problem of verisimilitude, of whether we measure the truth of our stories against some formal discursive or logical standard, or judge their worth in terms of how well they resolve the existential tensions, emotional double binds, and intersubjective complexities of human existence—in brief, how our stories and theories make our lives and ideals coincide.

But surely negative coincidences have also to be considered? Stories of imperfect or "harmful" coincidences,[2] of asynchrony and disharmony, in which there is no comforting sense of connectedness between the person we once were and the person we became or the place we began our life and the place we wound up in. In this regard, consider W. G. Sebald's recurring themes of *Unheimliche Heimat* ("strange homeland") and *Die fremdgewordene Heimat* ("the home country grown strange"), and the uncanny connection between estrangement from country and unrequited love.[3]

That the elegiac mood of Sebald's writings touches me so deeply is undoubtedly connected to my own ambivalent relationship with my homeland, for whenever I return to New Zealand, I experience the place as both utterly familiar and utterly strange. This feeling is undoubtedly exacerbated by jetlag and by transitioning, within the space of a day, from winter to summer.

A few years ago, having just arrived in Auckland on an early morning flight from Los Angeles, I stood in my sister's living room, transfixed by the sight of the distant Waitakere ranges and the white cumulus clouds that floated above them like puppets in a Balinese shadow play. On my flight across the Pacific, I had slept fitfully, my mind mired in a Sargasso Sea of disconnected memories from when I lived in New Zealand or first went to Sierra Leone. Now, walking out into the sun-drenched streets, I was borne back into the past, experiencing the agoraphobia that Auckland's single-storied suburbs always induce in me, with their weatherboard houses and mown lawns overwhelmed by an isthmus sky. Pōhutukawas, jacarandas, cabbage trees, and privet hedges were in flower. The air was heavy with the peppery, spermy odors of pollen and shrill with the brouhaha of birds, piping, whistling, and warbling. All this intensified the oppressive familiarity of the neighborhood in which I nevertheless felt like a stranger. This feeling deepened as I approached the house where my parents had lived until their deaths, the trees they had planted now felled, the lot now concreted over, and the house sitting in the middle of this desolate space like a dog kennel. Occasionally someone would drive down the street in a car, or emerge from a driveway, or an elderly person would pass me without a glance, lugging a shopping bag. But mostly the place was deserted, its life confined behind curtained windows and locked doors.

For several days I was haunted by the past. Or perhaps I should say I was haunted by its unreality. Though stirred to scribble poems about the harsh marine light, the smells that assailed my nostrils, the deafening birdsong, the white clouds, or the old photographs and family letters that my sisters kindly copied for me, I found myself struggling like a diver in the depths, desperate to surface and breathe fresh air, to embrace something new. Auckland belonged to another life, a previous reincarnation, or to someone else. Walking along Dominion Road, I marveled at how confused and lost this other "me" had felt forty-five years ago, riding home on the late-night bus, his head full of poems of unrequited love and the longing to get away. Back then, I had my whole life ahead of me. Now I was entering my *troisième âge*. In another twenty years, perhaps, I could well be like my mother who, in her early eighties, began a journal in which she set down reminiscences of her childhood and youth in the Taranaki town where she was raised. She told me at the time, "At my age you don't have a lot to look forward to, so you look back." At what age, I asked myself, does one cease to have a future? At what age is rebirth no longer possible? I suppose a lot depends on what the world offers you. In Sierra Leone I met young men who felt that the world offered them very little. Some of my contemporaries, recently retired, found themselves at loose ends and complained about the things they had dreamed of doing and had not done, while others, following in the footsteps of Milton's "uncouth swain," were moving on to fresh fields and new pastures. The repercussions of being born to particular parents, in a particular place, at a particular time, and what it means to be born to oneself, elsewhere, and with others, perplexed and preoccupied me throughout my sojourn in Auckland.

In connection with some research I was doing on Māori responses to genetic modification, I had made an appointment to see Manuka Hēnare at the Business School, located on the corner of Anzac Avenue and Short Street. I thought I knew the streets near the university, but was soon disoriented and had to ask for directions. A young woman was coming up Grafton Road toward me. I asked her if she could direct me to Anzac Avenue. She pointed down Symonds Street toward the harbor. It was in that direction, a couple of blocks after the High Court. She was walking that way herself and could show me.

She spoke with a North American accent, and I asked if she was from the United States or Canada.

"Canada," she said.

"Are you studying here?" I asked.

"No, I teach at the university."

I felt foolish. To someone in their twenties anyone over forty is old; to someone in their sixties, anyone younger than forty is young. "What do you teach?" I ventured to ask as we strolled along, hopeful that my sincerity would atone for my gaffe.

"Philosophy," she said.

"What kind of philosophy?" I asked. I was beginning to think I should stop bothering her; I now had a fair idea where the Business School was and should simply cross the road and make my way there alone.

"Twentieth-Century French and German," the young woman said.

Astonished by this coincidence of our academic interests, I told her that I was an avid reader of Walter Benjamin's essays and had, on the anniversary of his death, followed his ghostly and overgrown trail across the Pyrenees. I then asked which philosophers she had a particular interest in.

"Levinas," she said, and explained that she was writing a book about birth, time, and ethics. When she mentioned that it included a critique of Hannah Arendt's concept of natality I was flabbergasted. The chain of coincidences was too improbable. In Harvard Yard such an encounter might be expected. But Auckland, New Zealand? This was not the Auckland I remembered.

This exchange was so bizarre that it quickly eclipsed all sense of where I was and my meeting with Manuka Hēnare in quarter of an hour. Without hesitating, I asked the young woman how she reconciled Arendt's apparent attribution of agency to people—our capacity for initiating the new, for breaking free from the past and creating a future—with her repeated observations that human agency is almost nonexistent, and that our actions so exceed our intentions that we do not know, at any given moment, what we are doing or what its repercussion might be.

"Natality is not really a theory of agency," the young woman said. "Arendt is simply observing that the new arises continually in life, despite our plans, our intentions, our desires." At that moment, no one could have been more surprised by the unintended and contingent nature of new departures. But we had reached an intersection and the parting of the ways. As the pedestrian light changed to green, we stepped onto the crossing together, as if on the same course.

On the other side of the road, I said, "Well, I think I go this way now, don't I?"

"I'm going the same way," she said quickly. "The Philosophy Department is in Waterloo Quadrant. I can show you where you need to go."

As we walked on, she asked me where I was from.

I explained that I was in Auckland for three weeks, giving some talks at the university.

She appeared to relax a little. "Are you the person giving that public lecture on quandaries of belonging?"

"Guilty as charged."

"One of my closest friends here is in anthropology. Another recent arrival. She specializes in violence . . ."

"I've been writing on violence, too. I'd like to meet her." Most of all I wanted to know what this young woman felt about teaching continental philosophy in Auckland and living so far from home.

"It can be difficult sometimes," she admitted. "Only a few people with whom one can really share one's intellectual interests. The feeling of isolation."

She was amused when I told her that I had grown up in New Zealand feeling the same way, even though it was my homeland. "All through my childhood I had this fantasy that a mistake had been made and that I had been born in the wrong place at the wrong time, that another life awaited me elsewhere, and that if I was patient for long enough I would find it."

We had now reached my destination, and she rummaged in her bag and took out her business card. *Lisa Guenther BA Bishop's Univ, Ph.D Toronto. Lecturer.* "It would be nice to have lunch one day, if you're free," she said.

"That would be nice," I said. "I'll give you a call."

But I didn't; I got carried away by the research I was doing, distracted by the talks I had to give and the many old friends I wanted to see.

It wasn't until I had returned to the United States that I wrote Lisa, saying how much I had enjoyed talking to her, and expressing amazement at the serendipity of our encounter and our common interests. In response, she sent me a couple of chapters from her forthcoming book.

Lisa begins by observing that while it is practically impossible to remember one's own birth, it is often even more impossible to accept the fact that we did not choose it but came into existence in passivity, dependent on our parents, thrown into a world made by others at other times. While I had tended, in my own writing, to emphasize the ways we resist the overwhelming givenness of the world, gradually coming to define our own sense of who we are and often ritually renouncing that which was imposed on us in the first place without our knowledge and consent, Lisa's point of view reminded me of the positive dimensions of what is given to us, for it holds the potential of what we may become and foreshadows the ways in which we realize ourselves in intersubjective encounters with others—in conversation, and in sharing stories. Though Hannah Arendt stresses natality solely as the advent of a new person or the making of a new beginning,[4] natality is actually double-edged, since the new emerges both in the course of one's involvement with others and in one's awareness of being different from them. These two dimensions of natality—identity and difference, engagement and estrangement—find expression in quite different kinds of narrative. The first recounts who we are in relation to others, particularly those who give us life, while the second recounts who we are in our own eyes, when displaced or standing alone. Of our first birth we know little except through the stories and anecdotes our parents pass on to us, introducing us to our ancestry and satisfying our curiosity about our earliest and unremembered years. Sometimes it is possible to overcome the sense of unreality that clings to our own birth by having recourse to documentary evidence. Thus, Marguerite Yourcenar, researching her memoirs, describes how she was "forced"—just as if she "were trying to recreate some historical personage—to seize on stray recollections gleaned secondhand or even tenth-hand; to pore over scraps of correspondence and notebook pages which somehow escaped the wastebasket (so eager are we to know the past that we wring from these poor relics more than they contain); and to burrow in registries and archives for original documents whose legal and bureaucratic jargon is devoid of all human content."[5] By contrast, our second birth signals the beginning of the person we are for ourselves and the beginning of the life we will lead on our own initiative, and it builds on memories, designs, and desires that we like to imagine are all our own—a viewpoint famously captured in Simone de Beauvoir's pronouncement in *The Second Sex* that "one is not born, but rather one becomes, a woman; no biological, psychological or economic fate determines the figure that the human female presents in society."[6] But as Lisa Guenther observes in the introductory chapter of her book, we—which is to say we Westerners—sometimes find it difficult to accept that we never entirely outlive ourselves or that the past contains the germ and possibility of everything we may become. When she began writing her book, Lisa told me, she placed greatest emphasis on the first side of this aporia—"the unchosen particularity of existence," which in her case meant being born and raised in the suburbs of Winnipeg, Manitoba, Canada, "ardently hoping and almost believing that I had been left there by a troop of wild-eyed gypsies who were even now on their way back to get me and take them with them."[7] Gradually, however, her focus shifted to the critical events in her own life that marked new beginnings, new initiatives, and symbolic rebirths.

That Lisa's observations made such an impact on me was undoubtedly because I had in my own writing over many years been preoccupied by this tension between the ways in which we account for any human life in terms of what is pregiven—our culture, history, class, gender, and parent-age—and what emerges in the course of an individual life—from interactions and encounters with others, and from contingent events.

Marguerite Yourcenar's *Souvenirs Pieux*[8] emphasizes the pregiven and the preexistent. Like any other memoir, her narrative begins with the birth of an individual subject. "The being I refer to as *me* came into the world on Monday, June 8, 1903, at about eight in the morning, in Brussels." But after her first perfunctory paragraph, the author moves back in time, recounting her paternal and maternal family histories in such depth and detail that she is herself quickly eclipsed, and the subject of the memoir becomes, in effect, her maternal lineage. Yourcenar's avoidance of self-centeredness is, of course, deliberate. By freeing the personal *voice* from the conventional autobiographical burden of tracing the development and career of a personal *identity* she is better able to go "beyond the confines of individual history and even beyond History..." and explore "the hopeless tangle of incidents and circumstances which to a greater or lesser extent shape us all."[9]

Many of us like to tell the story of our lives as a series of lucky or unlucky breaks. Of fortunate or unfortunate coincidences. For Yourcenar, her life begins with the worst coincidence imaginable. Her mother dies in giving birth to her. As a result, the very possibility of her own existence is not her mother's life but her death. And while the daughter grows old, the mother remains forever young.

Perhaps this explains why Marguerite Yourcenar's historical biographies and fictionalized autobiographies refer constantly to the past, not out of nostalgia for a golden age, but because of the tragic connection between her own birth and her mother's death, and her awareness that her own life cannot really begin until her mother's life has run its full course. When Marguerite Yourcenar recounts her mother's story she (who is old enough now to be her mother's grandmother) symbolically inverts her relationship with Fernande and reverses the passage of time. Speaking of Fernande, Yourcenar observes that her memoir is an effort to "recapture and recount her history" and "fills me with a sympathy for her that I have not felt heretofore. She is much like those characters, imaginary or real, that I nourish with my own substance to try to make them live, or live once again."[10] In recounting what befell her in the past, Yourcenar acts imaginatively on events she suffered in passivity, symbolically bringing her mother back to life in order that she, the author, can lay her ghost.

This compulsive replaying of the past is, of course, definitive of trauma. People who have suffered abuse as children and have been deprived of any right to live life on their own terms will, as adults, repeatedly play back the situations that they suffered so passively, invading the space or exploiting the resources of others and even abusing or neglecting their own children as they attempt to reverse time and retrieve their own lost sense of agency.

Synchronicity is not something that happens to us, that we simply notice and wonder at; it is often something we play an active role in bringing about, much as we willingly suspend disbelief in order to be entertained by a conjuror or entranced by a storyteller. For the conjuror, like the storyteller, cannot perform his or her "magic" unless we are willing to be mystified by the sleight of hand, or disposed to focus on certain aspects of a coincidence and ignore details that might contradict our initial perception. Thus, even as we disavow the role we play in creating and interpreting events, we are continually looking for ways in which the world around us will confirm our assumptions and fulfill our expectations. A conspiracy theory, like the story of a remarkable coincidence, will often be framed with the phrase, "You won't believe this, but . . . ," and this "but" is the hinge of the story. It goes without saying that synchronicity strains credulity. But that is precisely where the existential meaning of synchronicity resides, because it allows us to fool ourselves into thinking that the impossible is possible. And without that hope, our lives would be unbearable.

Synchronicity involves a manipulation of time, which is why G. K. Chesterton compares it to punning (playing on words). It provides a satisfying illusion that we can call the shots in life, finding meaning where there may be none, seeing design where there is only contingency, conjuring hope in a hopeless situation.

Pierre Bourdieu observes that time is really experienced only when the quasi-automatic coincidence between expectations and chances, *illusio* and *lusiones*, expectations and the world that is there to fulfil them, is broken. We then feel directly the breaking of the tacit collusion between the course of the world—astronomical movements (such as the cycle of the seasons) or biological processes (such as aging), or social processes (such as family life cycles or bureaucratic careers), *over which we have less than full power or no power at all*—and the internal movements that relate to them (*illusio*).[11]

Synchronicity not only contradicts causality; it momentarily exchanges seriality for simultaneity. In this sense, a coincidence abolishes time. For a split second we are sustained by the illusion that different things are essentially alike, that separate persons, events, or entities are actually one, and even that we may achieve a state of timelessness and immortality.

When giving birth or attending a birth, one experiences time as compressed or condensed—as if nothing existed outside the moment in which this woman labors and the place where it is happening. One harbors one's resources, concentrates one's effort, focuses one's consciousness, and is intolerant of distractions. The everyday world seems a long way away. In these respects, confinement bears comparison with the experience of being with a loved one who is dying or being in a traumatic accident. Time seems to hang fire, annulled by the overwhelming immediacy of the event. But experiences of birth and death have something else in common: they are devastating to our sense of autonomy. A woman giving birth is in the grip of powerful forces she cannot readily bring under control. Drained of energy, maddened by her inability to master her pain, she can only yield to the demonic imperative of this other life that is tearing her apart as it forces its way into the world. Similarly, those near death and those who wait and watch them dying, are defeated by their helplessness in the face of something they cannot prevent. Perhaps this is why, at such times, we are mystified or outraged that the outside world is still going about its business, keeping to schedules and timetables, indifferent to our struggle for life, oblivious to our anguish. And yet, within moments of a birth or a death we begin, often despite ourselves, to reclaim the autonomy we momentarily lost, returning to the world, the dazzling daylight, the mundane activities we had momentarily lost sight of. In the stories we tell, whether to ourselves or to others, about what we suffered in passivity or silence, we recapture our sense of being able, if not to determine the way things are, at least to decide the meaning that is to be ascribed to them. Yet who can deny that for every story of a happy coincidence there's a story of an unhappy one, where expectations and chances did not converge, where the balance between acting and being acted on was catastrophically lost, when we found work but in the wrong place, met the right person at the wrong time, and there was no fit between the real and what we wanted the real to be.

Stories Happen

How many stories begin like this: "At 5.30
he set off from home to the corner store
saying he would be back by 6.00 . . . "?

You know immediately
that he never reached his destination
did not come back,
and that, between the poles
of home and world,
in a wilderness or city block
a story will be told and we will say, "If only"
or "Can you believe his luck?'

Yet everyone gets sidetracked
or overtaken or disappears. There's
always a traumatic or miraculous
encounter, waylaid by God
on a desert road or by someone
with whom you feel such love
you cannot tear yourself away.

When we recount the episode
we will say our life was changed
forever, that this was the worst
or best thing that ever happened to us,
as if we can divine the difference
between profit and loss,
add up the interest, the dividend
that accrued from taking one road rather than another,

our arbitrary decision now deemed fortuitous
as we with the wisdom of hindsight congratulate ourselves
for seeing our way clear, for not allowing
distractions to interfere
with our well-laid plans, authors
of our own destinies, who carefully plot
the life of our own character
as if one of the dramatis personae
that a playwright might bring together or force
to go their separate ways, knowing
what's good for them or pleasing to us
who like to guess what unfolded between x and y
or was on our hero's mind
when he turned at Lincoln instead of Dunne
answered a stranger's request for directions,
or crossed the street against the lights.

Affective Coincidences

The question of whether the past recurs in the present is perhaps less compelling than the question of *how* it returns and whether memory can explain all such recurrences. It is perplexing enough that events belonging to different times or places can mirror each other; the repercussions of such coincidences are often even more mysterious.

In her mid-sixties, my wife's mother embarked on a research project in the railway settlement of Frankton where her father had once worked as a railway porter and where she had spent most of her childhood. In the course of her fieldwork, Petra interviewed an elderly man who remembered her father. This man, whom I will call Arthur, confessed that he had nursed a grievance against Petra's father for forty years, having never been able to understand why, when his mother died, Petra's father refused to be a pallbearer at her funeral. As a close friend of the family, he had visited Arthur's mother when she was hospitalized and showed great concern for her recovery, so why should he turn his back on the family in their time of grief? Petra explained that her father had an almost pathological dislike of funerals. If he attended one, it was always with the greatest reluctance, and he would be rigid and unforthcoming for as long as the ordeal lasted. Petra had always seen her father's behavior in the light of his own father's death when he was eight. Two years later, Petra told Arthur, her father's little brother fell ill. The family lived in a remote rural district. They had neither a phone nor a vehicle. Their ten-year-old child was told to fetch the doctor. "Run to the doctor!" he was ordered, as if his brother's life was now in his hands. By the time the doctor reached the house, the child was dead. "You can imagine the impact of this experience on a ten-year-old child," Petra said.

When Petra recounted these details to me in 1994, a year before her own sudden death, she interrupted her story in order to find a photograph in her bedroom that she wanted me to see.

It is a black-and-white snapshot, dating to around 1929. It's late afternoon on a winter's day. A paddock in rural New Zealand. Long shadows extend from the pines, macrocarpas, and fences in the background. In the foreground, a family is flying kites. It is Petra's family. Her brother Bill has a diamond-shaped kite ready to launch into the wind. Bill's face is gaunt. He is still recovering from diphtheria, contracted during the recent epidemic. His brother Eric is, by contrast, outgoing and mischievous, and he has constructed a box kite out of bamboo strips, butcher's string, and old cotton sheets. Petra's mother is wearing a pinafore and holding her baby daughter in her arms. She is smiling at the scene.

When Petra puts the photo into my hands, however, it is not only her family that she wants me to see but also the figure of a man and his eight-year-old son in the background. The man is wearing a three-piece serge suit and he has placed his right hand on the little boy's shoulder. The boy is Arthur, the man Petra interviewed in Frankton, who had nursed a lifetime grievance against her father. That he is in this family photo, Petra says, is a sign of how close he was to our family. And she explains that she has had the photo enlarged and is giving it to Arthur, to apologize on behalf of her father, long deceased. To make amends.

Petra referred to her meeting with the elderly Arthur in the course of her fieldwork as a remarkable coincidence. That Arthur should figure in a family photograph taken one winter's day in 1929 was also, for her, a happy accident. But what I found compelling was not the improbability of these occurrences but what they entailed. How they initiated actions that redeemed a past slight or brought closure to a life story. In this perspective the traditional philosophical contrast between cause and coin-

cidence is illusory, for each of the events that came together as a coincidence had separate histories of cause and effect and subsequently led to
actions (Petra sharing her story with me and planning to give Arthur the
1929 photo in which he appeared) that the coincidence itself gave one no
inkling of. Any event both happens to us and is actively interpreted and
responded to by us. A coincidence is, therefore, not simply a matter of
chance, because the conditions of its very possibility and the consequences
of it reflect real life experiences that are anything but arbitrary.

It was only after transcribing Petra's story from the pages of my 1994
journal that I thought to read other entries I had made on that same day
of August 10. These entries were recollections of my mother's funeral,
which had taken place in Auckland a day earlier. After the funeral, my
wife and I, with our three-year-old son, had driven to Petra's place on
Whaingaroa harbor. Next day, walking alone on the iron sands of Ocean
Beach, with spume blowing from the open sea, and not a soul in sight,
my thoughts were focused on how my father would survive the loss of
my mother, and how my siblings would relate to one another now that
the most vital link between us had been lost. It then occurred to me that
Petra had shared her story of loss out of sympathy for my bereavement.
An affective coincidence, as it were, in which two independent histories
merged for a moment in a gesture of empathy.

When I turned north and retraced my steps to where the harbor
encountered the open sea, white water was seething and churning at the
bar under a sky of lowering cloud. At that moment I thought of the ancient
figure of the symbolon, a sign or token of something lying beyond our
immediate conceptual grasp yet a vital part of what we do comprehend. In
religious life this is the world of spirit as opposed to matter. For me, faced
with the ocean's turmoil at the harbor bar, it was the realm of raw emotion, breaking free of what I could put into words. I asked myself whether
these disparate realms could ever be made to coincide, to coalesce, a poem
capturing the grief that silences us, the spirit of a place glimpsed in cloud
shadows moving across a distant hill, a child's kite catching the wind, or
the world revealed in a wildflower.

Coincidence and Fate

In 1996, I resigned a professorship at Indiana University and returned to Australia to support my daughter who had graduated from art school only to find herself directionless and adrift. Having found a temporary half-time teaching position at Sydney University, I considered it only a matter of time before a more permanent arrangement would be negotiated. But within months of my arrival in Sydney, government funding cuts led to my contract being terminated. Though my professional situation was dire, my home life was happy. My daughter embarked on a teaching degree, and she was spending much of her free time with the children from my second marriage. I was also making new friends.

Souchou Yao had come from Singapore a year before my arrival from the United States, but he was finding it hard to get used to the bluster and discourtesy of our colleagues at the University of Sydney. As he struggled with culture shock, I was struggling to write a book that might bolster my chances of getting a tenured job. Consequently, we seldom interacted, though years later Souchou would recall us chatting at a faculty event, at which I confessed to having accepted the invitation in order not to offend the Head of Department on whom I was dependent for my continued employment. "I was taken aback by your candor," Souchou wrote in an email. "I was puzzled that this lion among his international peers, practically the sole architect of existential anthropology, was reduced to begging for academic crumbs."

It was only after I had left Australia that Souchou learned that a series of misfortunes, beginning with my first wife's death from cancer in 1982, had been partly responsible for my unsettled situation, and he surmised that my "quiet demeanor" not only reflected my backstory but also paralleled his own. "The deepest friendship," Souchou would tell me, "is not based on the sharing of good fortune but on the experience of unhappiness and social disruption."

My friendship with Souchou developed only gradually, during my return visits to Sydney and in the course of my research on his wife Simryn Gill's artwork. We shared the same ambivalent feelings about academe, and our ethnographic writings were similarly unorthodox.

In early 2019, I reviewed the manuscript of Souchou's *The Shop on High Street*, a book that subtly interweaves memories of his childhood experiences of working in his family's shop in Malaysia and an exploration of the philosophical, economic, and moral meanings of money (and the struggle to make money) in the context of Chinese petty bourgeoise life. In response to my praise of his work, Souchou asked what I was working on. When I mentioned my book about coincidence, he asked if he could read it, and he became particularly enthralled by my story of Renato/Renata, which reminded him of a personal story "from another time, another place. The plots are different," he said, "but the sense of fate or coincidence is uncannily similar."

At our house in rural Dabu, east of Guangdong Province, it was my grandmother's instruction never to turn away anyone who came to the door asking for food, water, or shelter in bad weather. This was before the Land Reform that came to our village in 1952.

Our house was a stopover for all kinds of people, including beggars, crazy-wanderers, priests going from temple to temple, petty traders on their way to sell their goods in the market town a half-day's walk away. One of our frequent visitors was Master Zhu, a Taoist monk with his trademark gray robe, walking staff, and begging bowl. My grandmother believed a monk's visit was propitious and giving alms was a virtue, so when Master Zhu came, she would get the maid to serve him food at the doorway. Tired, he would eat hungrily. Then my grandmother would press on him a few coins to send him on his way.

One day, after his meal, he asked to see the mistress of the house. When my grandmother came to the door, Master Zhu said, "I have a gift for you," and reaching into his cloth bag he pulled out a tiny puppy. Sleepy-eyed and dazed by the journey, the puppy came alive in my grandmother's hands. Master Zhu had picked it out of a litter at the temple, attracted by its wet nose and sparkly eyes, sure signs of intelligence in a dog. This gift was his way of repaying my grandmother for her kindness, he said, adding somewhat gravely, "It will look after the house and help you live through difficult times."

Old Yellow was the only pet I ever had. He was my friend throughout the years of land reform. One day, during the Kill all Pests Drive to raise production, all cats and dogs were ordered to be killed—because they were idle mouths, and because they spread disease. Old Yellow was one of the first to go. A servant put him in a gunny sack and drowned him. In my class at school, I proudly reported the patriotic act, but inside I was in despair. I have since been unable to look at a pet dog without a pang of guilt—for being there when Old Yellow died, for lacking the courage to confront the killers, for not begging my grandmother for its life, and for not remonstrating with the party cadres who supervised the murder.

The priest had said, "The dog will serve you well," and so it did, by dying. His death was followed by my grandmother's six months later. An era had ended; a new epoch of communism and the socialist paradise had begun. It prompted my father to decide that the family should now leave China. As for me, I am tempted to say the priest had seen in his mind's eye all that was to happen, including the future of the child he had appointed to be the master and companion of his gift.

Can I say that both my and your encounters with death tell the same story of fate, of unconnected events coming together, and of the power of death to teach us how to act ethically? My grandmother's charity sparked a series of events that led to our departure from China, just as your wife's death from cancer led to your decision to leave New Zealand and start over in Australia, and later move to the United States. All these events presaged our meeting in Sydney and the beginning of our friendship. A coincidence surprises us with its "out of the blue" quality, a quality we cannot fully account for. We struggle for words. And we are promiscuous in our search for a singular cause: fate, destiny, karma, god, the devil, the way of heaven. Almost any concept will do. But no matter how we think about coincidence, the phenomenon possesses a curious veracity for us and insists on being taken seriously.

In response to Souchou's story, I tried to summarize my book:

When I ask myself why people should assign deep significance to a coincidence rather than brush it aside as inconsequential, I am struck by the
degree to which suffering and anxiety increase not only our awareness of
patterns but our compulsion to find them. Another way to put this is to
say humans are meaning-making creatures. Whatever happens in our life
is given meaning in the way we respond to it, even when the form of our
response is culturally given rather than individually created. If this is true,
then a coincidence is never entirely a chance occurrence, but is one of the
ways in which we find meaning in life, defying the absurdity of existence and
the arbitrariness of fate.

Souchou responded with an anecdote from his fieldwork on Cheung
Chau Island, Hong Kong:

Chinese villagers often say, "Heaven has eyes." This expresses a fact and
serves as a warning. You twist your tongue when you say it, drawing out
the consonant in each word. *Tian* is heaven, but it also means "sky," which
gives the saying a strangely secular connotation. In fact, Heaven is simply
the most reliable witness to the joys and miseries of human existence. And
since god's all-seeing eyes register bad and good deeds alike, punishment is
meted out and rewards bestowed accordingly. In a fishing village on Cheung
Chau Island, people often say "Heaven has eyes." They say this when they
feel a wrong has been done to them, and they say it when they want to plead
to the gods for justice. But there are many reasons for the fishermen's anger
and sense of injury: a government meager with its assistance and subsidies,
money-grubbing marine engine dealers, diesel merchants given to hiking up
prices. People grumble about the land-based merchants' greed and wicked-
ness, but Heaven offers the assurance that things will be put right, and there
is still justice in the world.

   An anthropologist might ask whether these fisher-folk actually believe
the gods will do as they wish. But these are very practical people who know
that one's fortune or misfortune sometimes reflects the capriciousness of
the gods, sometimes the result of human failings, and sometimes can be
explained as fate.

   The Chinese word for coincidence is qiǎohé. The spirit of the word may
be translated as "ingenuous fit" (of events). But qiǎohé is a modern term,
like the word for oxygen or an element in the periodic table. Rural folk on
Cheung Chau are more likely to use the term *mingyun*, fate, or personal
destiny. When a marine engine breaks down in the midst of a storm, people
rant and rave, cursing everyone and everything. An adverse change in the

weather, a dealer suspected of selling a faulty engine, a merchant who has spiked the diesel with kerosene—all may be blamed. But while a merchant may be blamed for a malfunctioning engine, the weather is in the hands of the gods and you can't get angry with them for too long. If only for this reason, the island is dotted with temples, and the fisher-folk keenly participate in communal festivals. All this is to say that coincidence does little for the fishermen, emotionally or psychologically. The gods can be bribed, their anger can be pacified, but you still have to learn to rely on yourself.

This is, you might say, a pragmatic approach to fate and the will of the gods.

Fate is decidedly not unexpected; you may throw your hands in the air and say, "I am leaving everything to fate," yet the gesture does not preclude the importance of human agency. Just as the subjective and the objective are mutually entailed, so too is human effort and divine will. Each pairing interlocks the two elements like Lego blocks. And this is as true of philosophic thought as it is of everyday practice.

When you inveigh against logocentricity, it is important to remember that Chinese culture is profoundly anti-logocentric, and this spirit pervades all philosophical texts, including Confucianism, as well as everyday life and language. In Chinese, the words "subjective" and "objective" are literally, "the host's view" and "the guest's view" respectively. Experience is social, an interplay between the view of the host in, for example, a house meeting—because he presides over the proceedings and has the stronger say—and the guest—who is expected to hold back, observing the protocols but not dictating terms. The host-guest metaphor, however, does not imply an opposition between two ways of acting and thinking but emphasizes the complementary relationship between these different social perspectives. When I hear the Chinese terms for *objective* and *subjective,* I do not interpret this relationship in mutually antagonistic or either-or terms, but as a kind of transaction or negotiation. This principle or complementarity runs through all Chinese thought. Whether Heaven and earth, life and death, each element is a mirror of the other. Thus, papier mâché cars, houses, and credit cards are burned as offerings to the dead, that they may use them in the underworld. The tie that binds the opposites is sociality. Sociality ensures that subjective and objective views are not in conflict, that life and death, fate and personal initiative, are not negations of each other. It is a special kind of sociality, you might say. It is dialectical, it binds the opposites and yet each exists and operates in its own right. In Chinese thought, the things we desire—peace, familial harmony, prosperity, business profitability—are not to be taken for granted. In all these matters, individual will and heavenly dispensations make for a powerful and productive partnership.

Of all connections, the most complex and life-enhancing is the one between human subjectivity and the divine. But the conjunction—the awkward "between"—is misleading. It implies the union of two incompatible elements, as in a bad marriage. The concept of Zhong, or centering, offers a remedy. Instead of connection, zhong *coalesces* the mortal self and Heaven into a single, artful, and harmonious blending of opposites.

Zhong is an everyday concept. Honesty or interpersonal loyalty is zhong zin, "unwavering heart." But in traditional China, zhong is also a concept of imperial sacrifice, in which offerings were made to the gods to solicit blessings and good fortune for the people within the emperor's domain. It was a more majestic and spectacular ritual than the offerings to ancestors and the gods that people carried out at home. Yet, the aims and meanings were the same. To carry out a ritual is a perfect expression of one's ethical conduct that "moves even Heaven." In imperial sacrifice, the emperor is the most potent supplicant, the most legitimate messenger, who can traverse the metaphysical distance between heaven and earth. To reach Heaven may not be humanly possible, but it is certainly a communicative act, and the gods are "brought out" of their splendid isolation to cast their eyes on the secular world and its needs. Heaven and earth, nature and human society, are made one. As Angelo Zito writes, "Within this cosmos of transforming resonances, it remained vital for people not so much to 'join' nature (for this implies a separation) as constantly illustrate and display that there was not and had never been a gap."[1] For humble folk and the emperor alike, *li* ensures that messages get to the gods who, appeased and worshipped, will bestow their favors and benediction on the people. Here, it is necessary to understand the connotations of the concept *li*, which Angela Zito defines broadly as, "ways of being human that are considered necessary to the workings of the cosmos as well as its embedded social order, including everything from how to dress to how to venerate ancestors."[2] Thus, *li* refers as much to imperial sacrifice as to domestic worship or good manners. Everyone can attempt to reach the gods and perhaps secure a desired outcome. But in this process, ideas like chance and luck and coincidence begin to lose their relevance.

The trouble with the idea of coincidence is its presumptuousness. It denies the existence of a morally ordered universe. And without a morally ordered universe, life is bereft of tragedy. Tragedy evokes in us fear and pity, and pity—that excruciating empathy with others who are down on their luck—comes from our feeling that things shouldn't be this way. When the Chinese say "Heaven has eyes," they express the belief that even the worst that has happened to us is not without purpose or logic. But not everything in life reflects the power of Heaven, for an auspicious life requires one's own efforts as well as the occasional favors and indulgences of the gods. Chinese thought insists on the dialectics of earthly pursuits and heavenly blessings.

Abacus in one hand and joss stick in the other, though a cultural cliché, is not untrue. I like to believe that my understanding of Chinese thought resonates with your [Michael's] dialectical and ethical approach to philosophical anthropology. The burning question is the age-old one of how to live. There may be no way of reconciling our human aspirations with the powers beyond our control that help or hinder their realization, but in bearing witness to our experiences of living in the transitional spaces between the known and the unknown, the visible and invisible, we relearn long-standing lessons of existence and find common cause with others.

The Question of Verisimilitude

Martin Amis observes that, unlike narrative, life is poorly plotted, and suffers for want of good dialogue, pattern, or completeness.[1] Though we are constantly processing the bits and pieces of our everyday experience, turning them into stories, much as one periodically tidies one's house to avoid living in a mess, an inner voice reminds the storyteller that he or she is stretching the truth. But there are the truths we swear by, which are predicated on ideas of order, and the truths we glimpse through a glass darkly and cannot put into words.

I alluded earlier to the relationship between random events and meaningful conjunctions, and noted the improbability of our existence, both as a species and as individuals. It is astonishing enough that all our ancestors, from the first single-celled organism to our grandparents, survived to reproduce themselves, but when one considers that in a single ejaculation there are between 200 and 600 million sperm cells vying to fertilize a single ovum, the probability of a you or me being conceived is 1 in 400 trillion. While some might construe this as evidence that they were destined to exist, others might find such staggering randomness deeply humbling.

The question of whether our existence is a miracle for which we have the gods or Dame Fortuna to thank, or an accident that confirms our insignificance and makes us wonder whether there is much point to living and reproducing ourselves, seldom arises so starkly.

It is not that we are foolish when we read design and purpose into the history of our species or our genealogies, for it is our nature to find meaning in life, though there may be none. Nobody can live as a nobody. We need to experience ourselves as necessary, not accidental. Our being here must matter to somebody, even if it ceases to matter to ourselves. Something other than us must depend on our being here, in this place, at this time, even if it is only our children. We would not be human were this not so.

But was it so for the millions who met their deaths in the concentration camps of the Third Reich?

In *Man's Search for Meaning*,[2] more copies of which have been sold than the number of Jews who perished in the camps, Viktor Frankl writes that a hopeful and positive attitude contributed to his own survival in Auschwitz and subsequently inspired his development of logotherapy as a psychoanalytical technique. Is this a case of false memory? A salvage operation in which a person recovers his humanity by recounting a story in which he outwits those bent on his destruction? Even, perhaps, an example of Holocaust denial, for, as Primo Levi points out, "The 'saved' of the Lager were not the best, those predestined to do good, the bearers of a message: what I had seen and lived through proved the exact contrary: ... the worst survived."[3]

That Frankl's book became an enduring best seller may have had less to do with its verisimilitude than with our compulsive search for agency in life, even when there is little sign of it. The overwhelming evidence is that for most prisoners, they could say or do nothing to increase their chances of survival. And because meaning, in its most basic sense, implies being able to speak and to act, their lives were bereft of meaning. Stripped of all their possessions, including their names. Brutally separated from loved ones. Shorn. Silenced. Shut up. Beaten into submission. In this degraded and depersonalized state, life and death were matters of blind luck. Virtue, reason, will, talent, and even hope counted for little.

"Every survivor has a miracle story," writes Judith Sherman, who was fourteen when she was deported with her family from Czechoslovakia to Auschwitz. "How many trainloads were killed for that miracle?" she asks. "I do not know," she answers. "I do not want to know."

What she does want to know, and what she will continue to seek an answer for in the decades after Auschwitz and Ravensbrück and for all eternity, is why God allowed such things to happen.

"Are You not tempted, Lord, to intervene?" she asks. "God, do you not notice? They reverse Your Ten Commandments, they apply their own version to millions. Disposable millions . . . Do You notice?" A few pages later in her memoir, Judith describes the transfer to Ravensbrück.

> It cannot be, I say, and I am hit by a new evil, more terror, and I am still at the stage of being surprised by every new brutality. How can this be, I still say. "How can this be" is why people around me are in shock. Numbed. Uncomprehending, we react—but our reactions are for the world of "before"; they do not fit here.[4]

Primo Levi also addresses this experience of one's life reduced to mere contingency. When he finally returns to Italy after his year in Auschwitz-Monowitz, he is visited by a friend who tells him that his survival "could not be the work of chance, of an accumulation of fortunate circumstances (as I did then and still do maintain) but rather of Providence. I bore the mark, I was an elect: I, the nonbeliever, and even less of a believer after the season of Auschwitz, was a person touched by Grace, a saved man."

"And why me?" Levi asks.

"It is impossible to know," his friend answers. "Perhaps because you had to write, and by writing bear witness," and his friend asks whether Levi wasn't in fact writing a book about his imprisonment.

"Such an opinion seemed monstrous to me," Levi remembers. "It pained me as when one touches an exposed nerve, and kindled the doubt . . . : I might be alive in the place of another, at the expense of another; I might have usurped, that is, in fact, killed."[5]

Reading these testimonies to life in extremis, I am brought back to the perhaps unanswerable question: what on earth can one do, being a creature who *must* act, who *must* speak, when one is thrown into a situation that absolutely prohibits one to do or say anything except on penalty of death?

On his second day in Auschwitz, Elie Wiesel's father suffered a colic attack. Appealing to the barracks Kapo, he asked in polite German: "Excuse me . . . Could you tell me where the toilets are located?" The *block-*

älteste stared at the man for a long time, "as if," writes Wiesel, "he wished to ascertain that the person addressing him was actually a creature of flesh and bone, a human being with a body and a belly. Then, as if waking from a deep sleep, he slapped my father with such force that he fell down and then crawled back to his place on all fours."[6] In this hell on earth, there is nothing one can say or do that will affect one's fate. One's body—the body that craves food and sleep, that suffers lice and cold and pain—is a liability. As for one's soul, it is in ruins, for even almighty God does nothing, says nothing, gives no sign. Beaten and abused by SS guards, Judith Sherman asks, "God, how are we so visible to them and so invisible to You? You owe us visibility—."[7] And on the eve of Rosh Hashanah, as he hears thousands of lips repeating the benediction, Blessed be God's name, Elie Wiesel, who had once believed in salvation and prayer but now finds himself alone in a world that God has abandoned, asks, "Why would I bless Him? Because he caused thousands of children to burn in His mass graves? Because he kept six crematoria working day and night, including Sabbath and the Holy Days? Because in His great might, He had created Auschwitz, Birkenau, Buna, and so many other factories of death?" In such places, at such times, humanity is in the hands of those who have forfeited their humanity, while those who suffer, and are all too human, are stripped of everything that would suggest to their tormentors any kinship.

Though the prisoners are compared to animals, it is not ordinary animals that the SS have in mind—for these are useful and even loveable—but a degraded and useless species or collection of things—*figuren* or *stücke*, dolls, wood, merchandise, rags. "Move faster, you filthy dogs," the SS bellow. People are herded into cattle trucks. Police dogs tear a man apart. Those who survive become like animals, scavenging for a crust of bread, a scrap of cloth, a pair of shoes. Sometimes it is only an animal that is capable of recognizing the humanity of these degraded beings, as Emmanuel Levinas recalls, describing how, for a few short weeks during his long captivity, a stray dog entered the lives of the Jewish prisoners of war among whom he numbered. On their way to work in the forest each morning, the prisoners would be observed by German civilians in whose eyes, writes Levinas, we were subhuman, no longer part of the world. And then, one day, this cur that lived in some wild patch near the camp came to meet the pitiable rabble as it returned under guard from the forest.

This happened many times, the dog greeting the prisoners at their dawn assembly and on their return from work, jumping up and down and barking with delight. "For him, there was no doubt that we were men."[8]

Perhaps the most urgent question is not the question of what a prisoner could say or do inside the Lager, but what, if one happened to survive, he or she could say or do afterward. Elie Wiesel finds it difficult to answer this question. "Did I write so as *not* to go mad," he asks, "or to *go* mad in order to understand the nature of madness? Was it to testify to events we must never forget, lest they happen again? Or was it simply to preserve a record of the ordeal I endured as an adolescent, at an age when one's knowledge of death and evil should be limited to what one discovers in literature?"[9]

That these questions cannot be answered unequivocally attests to the poverty of our belief in our power to foretell our future or decide our own destiny. If I take any lesson from the testimonies of writers like Elie Wiesel and Primo Levi it is that human existence is largely a matter of contingency, not design, and that there are strict limits to our ability to know why things happen as they do or in what ways our words and deeds influence our unfolding lives. We like to imagine that we act rationally, or on principle—as if the ideas we hold in our heads are scripts that guide and even determine our behavior. But I have learned that we attribute reason and morality to our actions in retrospect, and that for the most part we act thoughtlessly, unconsciously, habitually, or despite ourselves.

What arrests me, reading these survivor tales, is not the brutality of the SS or even the fact of genocide (for despite all our dreams that things might be different after Auschwitz, history has decided otherwise)—but that *anyone* should survive that limbo that lay between memory and ash. Two days before the Red Army reached Buna, the SS evacuated the camp. In blinding snow, the thousands still able to walk were force-marched away from the front. Chilled to the bone, famished and at the very limits of their strength, these living dead were nonetheless able to march twenty kilometers, sometimes running, before being allowed to rest in a gutted brick factory. The dead lay in the accumulating snow like logs of wood. Yet the living pressed on, driven by the SS who shot whoever stumbled or fell. "Our legs moved mechanically," writes Elie Wiesel, "in spite of us, without us..."

It may be no more possible to find a reason for writing about such things than it is to explain why the majority of these prisoners did not give up the ghost but went on. One did so because this is what human beings do. This is what we do even when we see no reason for doing it or meaning in it.

Theodor Adorno writes that the Lisbon earthquake "sufficed to cure Voltaire of the theodicy of Leibniz." In the same vein, he argues that, "After Auschwitz, our feelings resist any claim of the positivity of existence as sanctimonious, as wronging the victims; they balk at squeezing any kind of sense, however bleached, out of the victims' fate. And these feelings do have an objective side after events that make a mockery of the construction of immanence as endowed with a meaning radiated by an affirmatively posited transcendence."[10]

Though the search for meaning may no longer serve as our guiding principle, whether as a way of identifying causes or discerning archetypes beneath the surface of events, we cannot desist from going back over the ground we have traveled, often in abject misery, and recounting our experiences. Even when our stories are about our powerlessness to act and our inability to understand, telling a story is itself empowering. It translates something private into a form that can be shared. It carries us beyond ourselves. This is why storytelling is as ubiquitous and inevitable as the actions of breathing, speaking, eating, and mating. We cannot help but search for meaning in what has befallen us, to restore our sense of agency when it has been overwhelmed by events we did not choose and could not control. Some speak of an obligation to bear witness to evil.[11] Others say that stories help us spell away the overhanging night or escape the ignominy and insignificance of our lives. But I think I agree mostly with Primo Levi when he speaks of the "small causes" in life when one chances to do one thing instead of another. Like Robert Frost, walking in the autumn woods behind his farm in Derry, New Hampshire, and coming upon a fork in the path. Taking one path because "it was grassy and wanted wear," as I did, years later, when I retraced Frost's steps in the same woods.

> I shall be telling this with a sigh
> Somewhere ages and ages hence:
> Two roads diverged in a wood, and I—
> I took the one less traveled by,
> And that has made all the difference

Coda

In *Minima Moralia*, Theodor Adorno speaks of "the impossibility of a coincidence between the idea and what fulfills it."[1] There is always a surplus or excess of being over knowing. This is as true of the idea of coincidence as it is true of our concepts of personality, nationality, and ethnicity. It is not simply the lack of fit between a concept and the lived experience it supposedly covers that concerned Adorno, but the danger of becoming so infatuated by an idea that we forget the singular individuals whose lives call every abstraction into question. Avoiding the subordination of people to ideas or the sacrifice of human lives to the false gods of ideology might be less urgent if it were simply a matter of striking a balance in academic writing between the general understandings we seek and the individuals, including ourselves, whose particular experience is at once the means and end of that understanding. But ideology enforces and reinforces social and racial divisions between those who deem themselves worthy of life and those they turn their backs on as unworthy of care.

Consider the notions of duty, law, and faith. Although these notions are often espoused as ultimate values, they can readily absolve us from the burden of thought since the thinking has already been done for us by God, or the ancestors, or an authority figure in whom we place our trust.

Hence, Adolf Eichmann's repeated assertion at his trial in Jerusalem, that he upheld the law and was a conscientious servant of the state. "He did his *duty*, as he told the police and the court over and over again; he not only obeyed *orders*, he also obeyed the *law*."[2]

I do not want to claim that dutifulness, obedience, or fidelity to a transcendent ideal is intrinsically incompatible with being a loving parent, a loyal friend, an ethical human being, or a good citizen. But swearing allegiance to a charismatic leader or a high ideal can, under certain circumstances, make one complicit in unspeakable deeds.

In Nuremberg in 1945, several high-ranking and well-educated members of the Nazi Einsatzgruppen (the mobile killing units on the eastern front) were tried for war crimes and sentenced to death. One of these men, Dr. Otto Ohlendorf, was found guilty of murdering ninety thousand Jews. In his defense, Ohlendorf argued that Hitler had good information that the Russians were planning to attack Germany. Since Hitler was better informed than he was, Ohlendorf was in no position to question this intelligence, and it was perfectly lawful for Germany to act in anticipatory self-defense. The chief prosecutor at this trial was a twenty-seven-year-old Jewish American lawyer, Benjamin Ferencz. Ferencz found Ohlendorf to be honest and rational, and in an interview some seventy years after the war he pointed out that the Pentagon would make the same argument today if it believed the United States was in danger of attack by a foreign power. By implication, history continues to repeat itself, and the ominous mantra that extraordinary situations call for extraordinary measures will be inevitably invoked to justify torture, mass incarceration of political enemies, the suppression of free speech, and the persecution of ethnic minorities.

In the same pessimistic vein, Ferencz observes that Ohlendorf was not incapable of humanity to his cats and dogs, his family, and the men under his command. The SS general did not believe in killing Jewish infants by bashing their heads against a tree. Instead, he told his men that an anguished mother should be allowed to hold her crying child against her breast. Then a single bullet would suffice to kill them both. This would spare his men from unnecessary distress and save bullets. It would also, presumably, lessen the possibility that the executioners should see their victims as human beings like themselves.

Perhaps because he did not want to be guilty of the same indifference as those whose crimes he was judging, Ferencz visited Ohlendorf in his cell shortly after his sentence had been handed down. The prosecutor hoped to better understand the mind of a mass murderer. Perhaps, too, he was worried that a desire for vengeance was affecting his professional commitment to due process. In any event, Ferencz soon experienced the same double bind that Hannah Arendt would experience sixteen years later after covering the trial of Adolf Eichmann in Jerusalem. To devote time and energy to understanding a person whose actions are unequivocally "evil" might be seen as compromising the judgment by finding mitigating circumstances or simply showing the "human side" of an alleged monster. Ferencz quickly discovered that Ohlendorf felt no remorse. "You'll see that I was right," he told the prosecutor. "The Russians will take over the Jews. The Jews in America will suffer." He then reiterated the arguments he had made to the court. Ferencz saw that nothing could be gained by continuing the conversation, and he ended it.

Reason without emotion is dangerous enough. But when entrenched ideas preclude the possibility of seeing other human beings as though they were oneself in other circumstances, reason becomes split not only from feeling but also from intersubjective reality.

It is all too easy to dismiss men like Ohlendorf and Eichmann as animals or monsters, as if everything about them is alien to us. Although Hannah Arendt regarded thoughtlessness "as a decisive...flaw in Eichmann's character,"[3] it is obvious from her painstaking account of his career that he was expert and efficient in applying his mind to the logistical demands of the Final Solution, and he gave considerable thought to how he could implement the Nazi plan to purify Europe of so-called inferior beings. It was not *thought* per se of which he was incapable, but *empathy*. He could not "think,...from the standpoint of somebody else."[4] It is impossible to disentangle this blindness to the humanity of others from his idealism. When the torturer is asked to account for his inhumanity toward his victims, he echoes the schoolmaster's words that this is going to hurt me more than you. The torturer sees the suffering of the other as an affront, and an assault on *his* personal sensibility. He is concerned solely with how he is affected by the sight of the other's torment. It is necessary to wring the truth out of this suffering prisoner, or kill these enemies of the state, and the only question is how the task can be performed with maximum efficiency—the records kept, the budget balanced, the orders followed, the quotas filled, the information gained, the deadlines met with the least amount of distraction from the human suffering this entails.

If, as Hannah Arendt argues, we focus on the "evil" character of Eichmann and his actions, we risk ignoring the conditions under which such characters come to power and such actions become possible. These preconditions are all too human: our ability for self-deception and bad faith, abnegating responsibility for our thoughts and actions because an allegedly higher power has approved them. Our propensity for granting an idea a greater value than a living person. Our short-term thinking, in which instant gratification for money, sex, or recognition precludes any consideration of the long-term repercussions of our acts. Our willingness to go along with what others are doing, or deem appropriate, avoiding the shame of standing out from the crowd or punishment for dissenting from the wisdom of the tribe. Our ability to forget what is not in our interest to remember and to remember only that which redounds to our credit. The list goes on. These may be the default positions for human beings. But are they symptomatic of thoughtlessness, or rather modes of thought in which all sense of intersubjectivity has been distorted, suppressed, or lost?

Not all thoughtlessness can be condemned. Some of the most generous human beings give to others without a second thought, while some of the most academically brilliant people appear bereft of empathy. Moreover, the demands of everyday life often leave us no time to think, or even feel. Recalling his experiences as a soldier before being recruited as a researcher and prosecutor at Nuremberg, Benjamin Ferencz says, "I didn't stop to think what's my emotional state. I asked myself what's next. Move, move...there's no time for emotion, no time for being shocked, for tears"[5] When collecting evidence of war crimes in liberated concentration camps, he speaks of setting up his office and building "a screen before my mind, to say this is not real...I was ice cold. I didn't shed a tear. I did my job, because that was my job, and to get out as best you can." It goes without saying that though Ferencz's state of mind may be compared with Ohlendorf's—since both men were struggling to do their work effectively under stressful and distracting circumstances, the former was humane and the latter inhumane. But it is important not to let our moral judgment about who is right and who is wrong blind us to the existential conditions that are anterior to morality and reflection. The soldier who goes to the rescue of a fallen comrade under fire and is subsequently awarded a purple heart for valor, often downplays his action, claiming that he acted without forethought and did what anyone would have done under the circumstances. Such protestations uncannily echo Eichmann's plea that he had no personal animus toward Jews, that his role in the Final Solution was an accident, and that almost anybody could have taken his place.[6] Beyond the fact that the soldier's "heroic" action saved a life and Eichmann's "evil" actions led to the deaths of millions, we must reckon with the fact that much human action is automatic and unreflective. If there is a "word-and-thought-defying *banality of evil*"[7] there is surely also a word-and-thought-defying banality of goodness.

Would that a single exceptional instance of goodness prove that a general rule of goodness exists. Unfortunately, this is more often the case in art than in life.

Florian Henckel von Donnersmarck's 2006 film, *The Lives of Others*, is set in East Germany in the years before Glasnost, the breaching of the Berlin Wall, and the reunification of Germany. A Stasi captain is ordered to place a playwright called Georg Dreyman under surveillance. While there is no evidence that Dreyman is involved in subversive activities, the order is given by the Minister of Culture who has designs on Dreyman's girlfriend. The Stasi captain, whose private life is lonely and loveless, monitors the intimate conversations and lovemaking of the couple from the attic of their apartment building. Gradually, his objectivity becomes compromised by his voyeuristic involvement in his subjects' lives, so that when evidence emerges that Dreyman is the principal author of a tract recently published in *Der Spiegel*, the Stasi captain prevents this information coming to the notice of his superiors. When other sources begin to reveal Dreyman's underground activities, the captain is able to destroy the typewriter hidden beneath the floorboards of Dreyman's apartment. Without this evidence, the playwright cannot be brought to trial. Several years pass before Dreyman accesses his Stasi files, learns about the years of surveillance, and realizes that his lover betrayed him to the Stasi and that the man responsible for collecting evidence against him actually saved his life. The playwright publishes a memoir and dedicates it to this man, HGW XX/7.

It is not only under totalitarian regimes that individuals are judged as being either for the state or against it, though such regimes exemplify a categorical way of thinking in which a human life is reduced to a single identifying characteristic. Nor is it even a matter of loyalty to the state, or the nation's supreme leader, for both the state and the leader embody an ideal, and it is to this ideal that people are made secondary and rendered superfluous. A person's sole duty is toward the realization and maintenance of the ideal. Unlike the abomination of slavery, in which a person becomes a chattel, the abomination of totalitarianism is that everyone becomes a slave to an abstract idea.

What happens in *The Lives of Others* is that one person recognizes (one might almost say remembers) that the person he has been given power over is someone he would like to be. Without consciously seeking to do so, he puts himself in the place of another. At first voyeuristic, gradually this identification becomes sympathetic.

For the idealist, whether religious or political, the idea to which he is attached is always transcendent. As such it cannot be questioned by a mere mortal, and its summons cannot be ignored. One has no choice in the matter. The idea carries its own necessity, whether this be the law of history, the law of nature, or the law of God. The idealist vows that he would give his life to the realization of the ideal. Ironically, he does not realize that he gave up his life the very minute he embraced the ideal as supreme or sublime.

When thinking becomes totally self-absorbed *or* fixated on an abstract idea, it becomes potentially as dangerous to self as to others. Although Hannah Arendt subscribes to Plato's idea that thinking is essentially talking to oneself (*eme emautō*), this intrapsychic two-in-one is inseparable from the action of talking to others, in which interior monologue becomes a dialogue between people.[8] This interplay between what goes on in the privacy of one's own mind and what transpires in the course of conversations and exchanges with others is suggested by her phrase, "the coincidence of thinking and thanking."[9]

The question of whether and in what ways the life of the mind ever coincides with the life we lead with others has been central to this book. To explain a coincidence in terms of unconscious forces or archetypal forms is to assume that inchoate ideas generate events. By contrast, we might argue that events are more random than we like to think, and though we are continually ascribing meaning to events after they have occurred, life is continually outstripping our efforts to comprehend or control it. For Hannah Arendt, the very idea that we are the authors of our own fate is questionable. Although we recount our histories as we recount our lives— as narratives of good and bad choices—"the real story in which we are engaged as long as we live has no visible or invisible maker because it is not made."[10] Although stories require agents, who make things happen and to whom things happen, in reality we act and speak without ever being arbiters of our destinies or lives, and history is "an endless new chain of happenings whose eventual outcome the actor is utterly incapable of knowing or controlling beforehand."[11]

There appears to be a contradiction here between Arendt's view in *Eichmann in Jerusalem* that we can be called to account for our actions, and the argument she makes in *The Human Condition* that all human action reflects a plethora of often competing influences, interests, and persuasions that are the outcome of *previous* experience, and that have ramifications that go far beyond what any actor knows, desires, imagines, says or does. The "simple fact," she observes, is that "we don't know what we are doing when we are acting," and we can neither grasp, practically or intellectually, "the manifold influences that bear upon us or the future implications of what we do."[12] This is not to reduce human existence to contingency, for our lives would be unthinkable without at least the *ideas* of agency and design. What Arendt wants to emphasize is the fact that human action always involves more than a singular subject; it occurs within fields of *inter*action that she calls the "subjective in-between." Accordingly, whatever anyone does or says is immediately outstripped by what others do or say in return. Every action calls out a reaction that "strikes out on its own and affects others."[13]

The resolution of this apparent contradiction between being responsible for our actions and being in thrall to circumstances beyond our comprehension and control lies in the recognition that both perspectives are entangled in any event. Thus, when a coincidence occurs, we are often undecided about whether a meaning inheres in the event or we have ascribed meaning to it in retrospect. It is the same with history and biography. Every critical event is inherently ambiguous, and it is often impossible to decide whether we can be blamed for having made a bad choice or forgiven because we were victims of circumstance, our passions, or the baleful influence of someone else. This ambiguity accounts for why Hannah Arendt can hold Eichmann accountable for his crimes while dismissing him as a clown or a sociopath. Finally, however, we are called on neither to explain or exonerate but to find the means of recovering life in the face of loss. Of starting over. This, Arendt writes, is the meaning of forgiveness, which implies neither loving those that hate us, nor absolving them from their crime, nor even understanding them ("they know not what they do"). Rather, it is a form of redemption in which one reclaims one's own life, tearing it free from the oppressor's grasp, and releasing oneself from those thoughts of revenge and those memories of one's loss that might otherwise keep one in thrall to one's persecutor forever.[14]

These strategies, she says, reflect the fact of natality—the power of action to bring the new into being. Thus, when we recount a story about any event that has befallen us, we play down the boundless field of influences and consequences that impinge on us, thereby creating the impression that our lives and histories are, at least to some extent, ours to have and to hold.

So it is with a coincidence. We are always in two minds about whether it holds a key with which we can unlock the secret of our lives or is random and devoid of any significance. As such, a coincidence encapsulates the ambiguity of human existence, for while life would be unbearable without meaning, we have no way of knowing for certain whether the meanings we invest in are true or false, harmful or harmless, and the relationship between ideas and life remains as indeterminate and mysterious as the relationship between two events happening to occur at the time in the same place.

Acknowledgments

I thank Duke University Press for permission to reprint the following:

"Ships That Pass in the Night" was originally published in *The Palm at the End of the Mind.* © 2009, Duke University Press. Reprinted by permission.

"The Other Portion" was originally published in *The Palm at the End of the Mind.* © 2009, Duke University Press. Reprinted by permission.

I also wish to acknowledge two other previous publications of mine from which material has been excerpted:

"As Time Goes By" was originally published in *Pieces of Music*, 1994, Vintage (Auckland). Author holds copyright.

"Amazing Grace" was originally published in *Pieces of Music*, 1994, Vintage (Auckland). Author holds copyright.

"Magdalene of the Black Rose" was originally published in *The Accidental Anthropologist*, 2006, Longacre (Dunedin). Author holds copyright.

Notes

PREFACE

1. Andrea Davies, "Convergent Narrative Structure: Where the Personal Meets the Political," Solstice MFA in Creative Writing Program of Pine Manor College, 2015.

2. James Baldwin, *Notes of a Native Son* (Boston: Beacon Press, 1985), 85.

3. Michel Foucault, *The Order of Things: An Archaeology of the Human Sciences* (London: Tavistock, 1974), 326.

4. C. G. Jung, "Synchronicity—An Acausal Connecting Principle," in *The Collected Works of C. G. Jung*, vol. 8, 2nd ed., trans. R. F. C. Hull (Princeton, NJ: Princeton University Press, 1969), 441.

5. Paul Ricoeur, *Freud and Philosophy: An Essay on Interpretation*, trans. Denis Savage (New Haven, CT: Yale University Press, 1970), 32.

6. Foucault, *Order of Things*, 326.

7. D. W. Winnicott, *Playing and Reality* (Harmondsworth: Penguin, 1971), 3, emphasis in text.

8. C. G. Jung, Foreword to the "I Ching," in *The Collected Works of C. G. Jung*, vol. 11, trans. R. F. C. Hull (Princeton, NJ: Princeton University Press, 1969), 587–608, at 592. Compare also with Jung's definition of synchronicity as "the simultaneous occurrence of a certain psychic state with one or more external events which appear as meaningful parallels to the momentary subjective state." Jung, "Synchronicity," 417–519, at 441.

9. As John Dewey puts it, experience "recognizes in its primary integrity no division between act and material, subject and object, but contains them both in an unanalyzed totality." John Dewey, *Experience and Nature* (New York: Dover, 1958), 8.

10. Limor Samimian-Darash and Paul Rabinow observe that new modes of risk, danger, and uncertainty are continually making their appearance (consider, for examples, contemporary anxieties over the dire effects of climate change, viral epidemics, or the rising threats of terrorism). At the same time, new modes of alleviating anxiety, reducing risk, and "taming uncertainty"—ritualistic, religious, and scientific—are continually arising as human beings struggle to makes their lives comprehensible, controllable, and bearable. Afterword to Limor Samimian-Darash and Paul Rabinow, eds., *Modes of Uncertainty: Anthropological Cases* (Chicago: University of Chicago Press, 2015), 203–7.

11. Or works written under the influence of Jung, such as Arthur Koestler's *The Roots of Coincidence* (New York: Random House, 1972).

12. "In the course of its evolution every science is periodically obliged to consider certain phenomena, or certain attributes of its subject matter, which seem to have a special meaning, not fully understood in terms of the characteristic methodology of that science." George Devereux, "Extrasensory Perception and Psychoanalytic Epistemology," in *Psychoanalysis and the Occult*, ed. George Devereux (London: Souvenir Press, 1974), 16–46, at 16.

A WORLD IN A GRAIN OF SAND

1. . Ranginui Walker, *He Tipua: The Life and Times of Sir Aprirana Ngata* (Auckland: Penguin2002), 55.

2. Susan Lipselter, *The Resonance of Unseen Things: Poetics, Power, Captivity, and UFOs in the American Uncanny* (Ann Arbor: University of Michigan Press, 2016).

3. Jerome Bruner, *Making Stories: Law, Literature, Life* (Cambridge, MA: Harvard University Press, 2002), 5.

4. Ann Taves, *Religious Experience Reconsidered: A Building Block Approach to the Study of Religion and Other Special Things* (Princeton, NJ: Princeton University Press, 2009).

5. Agehananda Bharati, *The Light at the Center: Context and Pretext of Modern Mysticism* (Santa Barbara, CA: Ross-Erikson, 1976).

6. Hent de Vries, *Philosophy and the Turn to Religion* (Baltimore: Johns Hopkins University Press, 1999), x, 5–6. De Vries acknowledges his debt to Derrida's critique of a "globalatinized," Greco-Roman bias in our thinking about religion. See, for example, Jacques Derrida, "Faith and Knowledge: The Two Sources of 'Religion' at the Limits of Reason," in *Religion*, ed. Jacques Derrida and Gianni Vattimo (Stanford, CA: Stanford University Press, 1998), 4, 30.

7. Mattijs van de Port, *Ecstatic Encounters: Bahian Candomblé and the Quest for the Really Real* (Amsterdam: Amsterdam University Press, 2011), 18.

8. Devaka Premawardhana, "Between Logocentrism and *Loco*centrism: *Alambrista* Challenges to Traditional Theology," *Harvard Theological Review* 101, no. 3–4 (2008): 399–416, at 401; Edward W. Said, *Humanism and Democratic Criticism* (New York: Columbia University Press, 2004), 47.

9. Michael Jackson, *The Palm at the End of the Mind: Relatedness, Religiosity, and the Real* (Durham, NC: Duke University Press, 2009), xii.

10. William James noted, since "whatever it may be on the *farther* side, the 'more' with which in religious experience we feel ourselves connected is on the *hither* side the subconscious continuation of our conscious life." *The Varieties of Religious Experience* (New York: Signet, 1958), 386.

LOST AND FOUND

1. Julian of Norwich, *The Writings of Julian of Norwich: A Vision Showed to a Devout Woman and a Revelation of Love*, ed. Nicholas Watson and Jacqueline Jenkins (University Park: Pennsylvania State University Press, 2007), 125–29.

2. Devaka Premawardhana, "Between Logocentrism and *Loco*centrism: *Alambrista* Challenges to Traditional Theology," *Harvard Theological Review* 101, no. 3–4 (2008): 399–416, at 401.

3. C. G. Jung, *Memories, Dreams, Reflections*, trans. Richard and Clara Winston (New York: Vintage, 1965), 51.

4. Vladimir Nabokov, "Translator's Introduction," in Mihail Lermontov's *A Hero of Our Time*, translated by Vladimir Nabokov with Dmitri Nabokov (Garden City, NY: Doubleday Anchor Books, 1958), x. Vladimir Nabokov observes that eavesdropping is "one form of a more general device which can be classified under the heading of Coincidence, to which belongs, for instance, the Coincidental Meeting."

5. This is characteristic of classical empiricism as well as a logocentric worldview, and it is relevant to point out that the root *log* from which *logos* derives means, among other things, "to gather," that is, "to pick out things which from some standpoint are alike." "It is precisely this emphasis on ultimate identity, on sameness or unity notwithstanding the possibility of penultimate differentiation, that had carried significant weight in the development of both philosophy and theology in the West." Premawardhana, "Between Logocentrism and *Loco*centrism," 401.

6. "Ethiopian Airlines: Two Men Say They Missed Crashed Flight," *BBC News Online*, March 11, 2019.

7. "Peter Ustinov Does Charles Laughton Impressions," YouTube, www.youtube.com/watch?v=u3nrhego1no, accessed October 13, 2020.

8. *Everything Is Copy: Nora Ephron Scripted and Unscripted*, HBO documentary, dir. Jacob Bernstein, 2016.

9. George Devereux, "Extrasensory Perception and Psychoanalytic Epistemology," in *Psychoanalysis and the Occult*, ed. George Devereux (London: Souvenir Press, 1974), 16–46, at 16, italics in text.

SYNCHRONICITY AND SUFFERING

1. Bernard D. Beitman, "Brains Seek Patterns in Coincidences," *Psychiatric Annals* 39, no. 5 (2009): 255–64.

2. Jennifer A. Whitson and Adam D. Galinsky, "Lacking Control Increases Pattern Perception," *Science* 322, no. 5398 (2008): 116–17.

3. C. G. Jung, "Synchronicity—An Acausal Connecting Principle," in *The Collected Works of C. G. Jung*, vol. 8, 2nd ed., trans. R. F. C. Hull (Princeton, NJ: Princeton University Press, 1969), 437.

4. Jung, "Synchronicity," 431.

5. In the *Symposium*, Plato has a pseudonymous Aristophanes claim that human beings originally combined male and female forms and possessed two faces as well as four legs and arms. When the gods became alarmed by the strength, power, and ambition of these creatures, Zeus decided to weaken them by cutting them in half, "just as people cut sorb-apples in half when they're going to preserve them, or cut an egg in two with a hair." But because the very "essence" of these androgynous beings had been sundered, each half now missed its complementary half and sought reunion with it. Zeus then conceived the plan of moving their genitals from the backs of their bodies to the front, thus enabling these divided beings to enjoy sexual union and procreate their kind. "Love," Aristophanes concludes, "draws our original nature back together . . . Turbot-like, each of us has been cut in half, and so we are human tallies, constantly searching for our counterparts." Plato, *Symposium*, trans. Robin Waterfield (Oxford: Oxford University Press, 1994), 25–28.

THE OTHER PORTION

1. Larry McCaffery and Sinda Gregory, "Interview with Paul Auster" (1989), in *Conversations with Paul Auster*, ed. James M. Hutchisson (Jackson: University Press of Mississippi, 2013), 13–14.

2. Paul Auster, *True Tales of American Life*, ed. and introduced by Paul Auster (London: Faber, 2001), xvi.

3. Auster, *True Tales of American Life*, xviii.

4. Virginia Woolf, *Moments of Being: Unpublished Autobiographical Writings* (London: Triad, 1978), 114.

CORRESPONDENCES

1. Claude Lévi-Strauss, *The Raw and the Cooked: Introduction to a Science of Mythology 1*, trans. John and Doreen Weightman (London: Jonathan Cape, 1970), 286, 297–98. See also, Alan Dundes, *Folklore Matters* (Knoxville: University of Texas Press, 1989), 104–6.

2. John Banville, "The Volcano Lover: A Romance," review in the *New York Times*, August 9, 1992.

3. R. F. Keam, *Tarawera: The Volcanic Eruption of 10 June 1886* (Auckland: R. F. Keam, 1988), 66.

4. Keam, *Tarawera*, 53–56.

5. Cited by Geoff Park in "Book Techtonics," *New Zealand Listener*, March 11–17, 1988, 40.

6. Keam, *Tarawera*, xiii.

7. Park, "Book Techtonics," 41.

SHIPS THAT PASS IN THE NIGHT

1. C. G. Jung, *Memories, Dreams, Reflections*, trans. Richard and Clara Winston (New York: Vintage, 1965), xii.

2. Deirdre Bair, *Jung: A Biography* (Boston: Little, Brown, 2003), 303.

3. Bair, *Jung: A Biography*, 302.

4. Richard Ellmann, *James Joyce*, new and rev. ed. (New York: Oxford University Press, 1982), 679.

5. I am echoing Hannah Arendt's notion of natality, the "character of startling unexpectedness [that] is inherent in all beginnings and all origins" and occurs "against the overwhelming odds of statistical laws and their probability, which for all practical, everyday purposes amounts to certainty." *The Human Condition* (Chicago: University of Chicago Press, 1958), 178.

CHANCE MEETING

1. Louis MacNeice, cited by Jeremy Adler in his afterword to Elias Canetti, *Party in the Blitz: The English Years*, trans. Michael Hofmann (London: Harvill, 2005), 230.

2. Canetti, *Party in the Blitz*, 232.

3. Elias Canetti, *Crowds and Power*, trans. Carol Stewart (New York: Farrar, Straus and Giroux, 1984), 275.

4. Canetti, *Party in the Blitz*, 196–97.

COINCIDENCE AND THEODICY

1. Ian Hacking (1990), cited by Natasha Dow Schüll, "The Gaming of Chance: Online Poker Software and the Potentialization of Uncertainty," in *Modes of Uncertainty: Anthropological Cases*, ed. Limor Samimian-Darash and Paul Rabinow (Chicago: University of Chicago Press, 2015), 46–66, at 47.

2. Marcel Griaule, "Notes sur la Divination par Chacal," *Bulletin de la Comité d'é tudes Historiques et Scientifiques de l'Afrique Occidentale Française*, 1937, cited in Lucy Mair, *Witchcraft* (London: Weidenfeld and Nicolson, 1969), 95–99.

3. Michael Jackson, "How to Do Things with Stones," in *Lifeworlds: Essays in Existential Anthropology* (Chicago: University of Chicago Press, 2013), 31–48.

4. John Dewey, *Experience and Nature* (New York: Dover, 1958), 44. See also John Dewey, *The Quest for Certainty* (New York: Perigee Books, 1980).

5. E. E. Evans-Pritchard, *Witchcraft, Oracles, and Magic among the Azande* (Oxford: Oxford University Press, 1976), 69–70.

6. Evans-Pritchard, *Witchcraft*, 70.

7. Barbara Bode, *No Bells to Toll: Destruction and Creation in the Andes* (New York: Scribner's, 1989), xxxvi.

8. Bode, *No Bells*, xliv.

9. Bode, *No Bells*, 99.

10. Bode, *No Bells*, 101–2.

11. Bode, *No Bells*, 175.

12. Bode, *No Bells*, 151–61.

13. Bode, *No Bells*, xliv.

14. Albert Einstein, *The Bohr-Einstein Letters* (London: Macmillan, 1971), 91.

AMAZING GRACE

1. Hannah Arendt, *The Human Condition* (Chicago: University of Chicago Press, 1958), 237.

2. Veena Das, *Critical Events: An Anthropological Perspective on Contemporary India* (Delhi: Oxford University Press, 1995), 139.

3. Das, *Critical Events*, 139–40.

ABOUT TIME

1. Richard N. Coe, *Beckett* (London: Oliver and Boyd, 1964), 28–29.

2. Drew Leder, *The Absent Body* (Chicago: University of Chicago Press, 1990).

3. Thomas Wolfe, *Of Time and the River: A Legend of Man's Hunger in His Youth* (New York: Scribner's, 1952), 60.

4. Marcel Proust, *Swann's Way, Part 1*, trans. C. F. Scott Moncrieff (London: Chatto and Windus, 1966), 3.

5. Don Bishop, "Tom Wolfe as a Student," in *The Enigma of Thomas Wolfe: Biographical and Critical Selections*, ed. Richard Walser (Cambridge, MA: Harvard University Press, 1953), 8–17.

6. Thomas Wolfe, "The Story of a Novel," in *Selections from the Works of Thomas Wolfe*, ed. Maxwell Geismar (London: Heinemann, 1952), 562–611, at 579.

7. Ernest Hemingway, *Green Hills of Africa* (New York: Scribner's, 1935), 72.

8. William Faulkner, *The Sound and the Fury* (London: Chatto and Windus, 1961), 74.

9. Wolfe, *Of Time and the River*, 51–53.

10. In traditional Kuranko stories from northern Sierra Leone, storytellers frame their tales as occurring long ago in a distant place only to intermittently remind their audience that the unfolding events are located in places familiar to them and, by implication, also occurring in the here and now. An ironic counterpoint is thereby struck between the fabled and the real, and it may be argued that this shuttling to and fro between past and present, myth and reality, is a strategy to draw the audience into a story that speaks directly to the ethical and emotional quandaries of their everyday lives as well as to bring home to them the ever-recurring issues of existential time. Brian Finney, "Temporal Defamiliarization in Toni Morrison's *Beloved*," *Obsidian* 11 (1990): 20–35, at 21.

11. H. M. Ledig-Rowohlt, "Thomas Wolfe in Berlin," *American Scholar* 22, no. 2 (1953): 185–201, at 186.

12. Anthony Kerrigan and Alastair Reid, "Editor's Epilogue," in Jorge Luis Borges, *A Personal Anthology* (London: Cape, 1968), 205–10.

MARCH 15, 2019

1. C. G. Jung, Foreword to the "I Ching." In *The Collected Works of C. G. Jung*, vol. 11, trans. R. F. C. Hull (Princeton, NJ: Princeton University Press, 1969), 587–608, at 592.

2. Johann Wolfgang von Goethe, *Elective Affinities*, trans. R. J. Hollingdale (Harmondsworth: Penguin, 1971), 52–53.

CONFLUENCES

1. Pierre Bourdieu, *Outline of a Theory of Practice*, trans. Richard Nice (Cambridge: Cambridge University Press, 1977), 163.

2. J. H. van den Berg, cited by Seth Barry Watter, "Scrutinizing: Film and the Microanalysis of Behavior," *Grey Room* 66 (Winter 2017): 32–69, 58.

3. Fiona Macdonald, "The Photos That Changed History," *BBC Culture*, September 14, 2017.

LOVE

1. Perkins slightly misquotes Virgil's *Aeneid: Et vera incessu patuit dea*, "and the goddess was revealed in her step," referring to Venus revealing herself before Aeneas. Rodger L. Tarr, ed., *As Ever Yours: The Letters of Max Perkins and Elizabeth Lemmon* (University Park: Pennsylvania State University Press, 2003), 25.

2. A. Scott Berg, *Max Perkins: Editor of Genius* (New York: Dutton, 1978), 386.

3. Tarr, *As Ever Yours*, 232.

IT SO HAPPENED THAT . . .

1. Georg Groddeck, *The Book of the It: Psychoanalytical Letters to a Friend* (New York: Nervous and Mental Disease Publishing, 1928).

CONTRIVED COINCIDENCES

1. Victor Turner, *The Forest of Symbols: Aspects of Ndembu Ritual* (Ithaca, NY: Cornell University Press, 1960), 105.

THE DOUBLE

1. C. G. Jung, *Four Archetypes*, trans. R. F. C. Hull (London: Routledge and Kegan Paul, 1972).

2. Joseph Campbell, *The Hero with a Thousand Faces* (Princeton, NJ: Princeton University Press, 1968).

3. Christopher Booker, *The Seven Basic Plots: Why We Tell Stories* (New York: Continuum, 2004).

4. Charles Stang, *Our Divine Double* (Cambridge, MA.: Harvard University Press, 2016).

5. Vladimir Nabokov, *Look at the Harlequins!* (New York: McGraw-Hill, 1974), 225.

6. Fernando Pessoa, *The Book of Disquiet*, trans, Richard Zenith (London: Penguin, 2002), 170.

7. Doug Wright, *I Am My Own Wife: Studies for a Play about the Life of Charlotte von Mahlsdorf* (New York: Faber and Faber, 2004), x.

8. Wright, *I Am My Own Wife*, xv.

9. Pessoa, *Book of Disquiet*, 327–28.
10. Pessoa, *Book of Disquiet*, 170.

CHINESE BOXES

1. Czeslaw Milosz, *History of Polish Literature*, 2nd ed. (Berkeley: University of California Press, 1983), 193.
2. Ian Maclean, Introduction to Jan Potocki, *The Manuscript Found in Saragossa*, trans. Ian MacLean (New York: Viking, 1995), xi–xviii, at xii. In 1905, a twenty-one-year-old Polish philosophy student, Bronislaw Malinowski, was awarded the Potocki Foundation stipend for Polish Noblemen, though the funds were insufficient to pay his way to England where he embarked on his career in anthropology in 1910.
3. Frank Bren, *World Cinema 1: Poland* (London: Flicks Books, 1986), 68.
4. Theodor Adorno, "On Subject and Object," in *Critical Models: Interventions and Catchwords*, trans. Henry W. Pickford (New York: Columbia University Press, 1998), 245–48, at 245.

AUTUMN LEAVES

1. Claude Lévi-Strauss, *Tristes Tropiques*, trans. John and Doreen Weightman (London: Cape, 1973), 376.
2. Lévi-Strauss, *Tristes Tropiques*, 376–77.

MAGDALENE OF THE BLACK ROSE

1. Blaise Cendrars, "The Art of Fiction," interviewed by Michel Manoli, trans. William Brandon, *Paris Review* 37 (Spring 1966): 105–32, cat. 118.
2. "Magdalene of the Black Rose," in Michael Jackson, *Duty Free: Selected Poems, 1965–1988* (Dunedin: McIndoe, 1989), 82–94.
3. Jorge Luis Borges, "The Dream of Coleridge," in *Other Inquisitions, 1937–1952*, trans. Ruth L. C. Simms (New York: Simon and Schuster, 1964), 14–17, at 15.
4. Blaise Cendrars, *L'Homme foudroyé* (Paris: Denoël, 1945). 265–66.
5. "Blaise Cendrars vous parle," Entretien premier and entretien cinquième. In *Oeuvres complètes*, vol. 8 (Paris: Denoël, 1964), 547, 599.
6. Miriam Cendrars, interview with Frédéric Ferney, Boulogne-sur-Seine, December 21, 1992. In Frédéric Ferney, *Blaise Cendrars* (Paris: Editions François Bourin, 1993), 134.
7. Ludwig Wittgenstein, *Tractatus Logico-Philosophicus*, ed. B. F McGui-

ness, T. Nyberg, and C. H. Wright (London: Routledge and Kegan Paul, 1922), last sentence.

ALL THE BIRDS OF THE AIR

1. C. G. Jung, "Synchronicity—An Acausal Connecting Principle," in *The Collected Works of C. G. Jung*, vol. 8, 2nd ed., trans. R. F. C. Hull (Princeton, NJ: Princeton University Press, 1969), 438–39.

THE RELATIVITY OF OUR VIEWPOINTS

1. Ernest Hemingway, *A Moveable Feast* (London: Arrow Books, 1996), 63.
2. Hemingway, *A Moveable Feast*, 63–64.
3. Lawrence Durrell, *Balthazar* (London: Faber and Faber, 1961), 14.
4. Hemingway, *A Moveable Feast*, 69–70.
5. Brassaï, *Henry Miller: The Paris Years*, trans. Timothy Brent (New York: Arcade, 1995), 172.
6. Georges Simenon, *Quand j'étais vieux* (Paris: Presses de la Cité, 1970), 365–66.

AS TIME GOES BY

1. Umberto Eco, *Travels in Hyperreality*, trans. William Weaver (Boston: Houghton Mifflin, 1990), 20.
2. Dante Gabriel Rossetti, "Sudden Light."

PIECES OF MUSIC

1. Norman Lebrecht, *The Book of Musical Anecdotes* (London: Sphere Books, 1987), 317.
2. Ned Wharton, "A 'Cosmic Connection' between Two Violinists," *NPR Music Interviews*, October 27, 2018.

THE LOST CHILD

1. David G. Wright, *Joyita: Solving the Mystery* (Auckland: Auckland University Press, 2002), 1.
2. Wright, *Joyita*, viii.

3. Wright, *Joyita*, x.

4. Wright, *Joyita*, xvi.

5. Wright, *Joyita*, 97.

IN THE NATURE OF THINGS

1. George Devereux, *Psychoanalysis and the Occult* (Madison, CT: International Universities Press, 1953), xi, 16–23.

2. Dilip M. Salwi, *Scientists of India* (New Delhi: Children's Book Trust, 1986), 133–45.

3. "Mentor Who Led Many to High Achievement," *Otago Daily Times*, March 31, 2018.

IL RITORNO IN PATRIA

1. Paul Auster, ed., *True Tales of American Life* (London: Faber and Faber, 2001), xviii.

2. See, for example, Guy de Maupassant's story "The Wreck," in which the protagonist, Georges Garin, suffers two harmful coincidences.

3. W. G. Sebald, *A Place in the Country*, trans. Jo Catling (New York: Random House, 2013).

4. Hannah Arendt, *The Human Condition* (Chicago: University of Chicago Press, 1958), 177–78.

5. Marguerite Yourcenar, *Dear Departed: A Memoir*, trans. Maria Louise Ascher (London: Virago, 1997), 4.

6. Simone de Beauvoir, *The Second Sex*, trans. H. M. Parshley (New York: Knopf, 1972), 295.

7. Lisa Guenther, *The Gift of the Other: Levinas and the Politics of Reproduction* (Albany: State University of New York Press, 2006).

8. Translated as *Dear Departed* (1997).

9. Elsewhere, she has noted: "It is *very important* that the reader *not* get the impression that the author is greatly or personally interested about her origins, since the whole quest is more sociological and historical than personal." Cited by Harold Beave, "Remembering the World She Never Knew," *New York Times Book Review*, March 1, 1992, 13.

10. Yourcenar, *Dear Departed*, 53.

11. Pierre Bourdieu, *Pascalian Meditations*, trans. Richard Nice (Oxford: Polity Press, 2000), 208–9, emphasis added.

COINCIDENCE AND FATE

1. Angelo Zito, *Of Body and Brush* (Chicago: University of Chicago Press, 1997), 101.
2. Zito, *Of Body and Brush*, 58.

THE QUESTION OF VERISIMILITUDE

1. Martin Amis, *Experience* (London: Vintage, 2001), 11.
2. Viktor Frankl, *Man's Search for Meaning* (New York: Washington Square Press, 1985).
3. Primo Levi, *The Drowned and the Saved*, trans. Raymond Rosenthal (New York: Vintage, 1989), 82.
4. Judith Sherman, *Say the Name: A Survivor's Tale in Prose and Poetry* (Albuquerque: University of New Mexico Press, 2005), 62, 65–66.
5. Levi, *The Drowned and the Saved*. 82.
6. Elie Wiesel, *Night*, a new translation by Marion Wiesel (New York: Hill and Wang, 2006). 39.
7. Sherman, *Say the Name*, 49.
8. Emmanuel Levinas, *Difficult Freedom: Essays on Judaism*, trans. Seán Hand (Baltimore: Johns Hopkins University Press 1990), 153.
9. Wiesel, *Night*, vii.
10. Theodor W. Adorno, *Negative Dialectics*, trans. E. B. Ashton (New York: Continuum, 1973), 361.
11. Primo Levi, *Moments of Reprieve*, trans. Ruth Feldman (London: Abacus 1987), 109–14. Primo Levi, *The Drowned and the Saved*, 174.

CODA

1. Theodor Adorno, *Minima Moralia: Reflections from Damaged Life*, trans. E. F. N. Jephcott (London: Verso, 1978), 176.
2. Hannah Arendt, *Eichmann in Jerusalem: A Report on the Banality of Evil* (London: Faber and Faber, 1963), 120.
3. Arendt, *Eichmann in Jerusalem*, 43.
4. Arendt, *Eichmann in Jerusalem*, 44.
5. *Prosecuting Evil: The Extraordinary World of Ben Ferencz*, produced and directed by Barry Avrich (Los Angeles: Seventh Art Releasing, 2018).
6. Arendt, *Eichmann in Jerusalem*, 255.
7. Arendt, *Eichmann in Jerusalem*, 59–60.
8. Hannah Arendt, *The Life of the Mind* (New York: Harcourt, Brace, 1978), 185.

9. Arendt, *Life of the Mind*, 186.

10. Hannah Arendt, *The Human Condition* (Chicago: University of Chicago Press, 1958), 186.

11. Arendt, *Eichmann in Jerusalem*, 59–60.

12. Arendt, *Human Condition*, 180.

13. Arendt, *Human Condition*, 190.

14. Arendt, *Human Condition*, 237.

Index

Founded in 1893,
UNIVERSITY OF CALIFORNIA PRESS
publishes bold, progressive books and journals
on topics in the arts, humanities, social sciences,
and natural sciences—with a focus on social
justice issues—that inspire thought and action
among readers worldwide.

The UC PRESS FOUNDATION
raises funds to uphold the press's vital role
as an independent, nonprofit publisher, and
receives philanthropic support from a wide
range of individuals and institutions—and from
committed readers like you. To learn more, visit
ucpress.edu/supportus.